Praise for NOURISH

"Mark's passion and determination to make a difference in the lives of millions of hungry children and families is amazing. This book is a culmination of his many years in the vineyard, and is quite inspirational."

—**Mary Landrieu,** former United States senator, Louisiana

"Mark Moore has proven that one person can make a dream a reality and help change the world for the better. With *Nourish,* he illuminates God's love in providing for us in a myriad of ways. This book is for everyone who is hungry and seeks to be nourished, and all those responding to the call to feed our brothers and sisters who are hungry."

—**Max Finberg,** former executive director, Alliance to End Hunger

"This is a book for the hungry. Mark's experience and adventurous spirit will feed that desire within each and every one of us to use our life in a way that makes life better for those around us. In a world that often attempts to segregate the spiritual from the secular, *Nourish* will challenge that notion, all the while inviting us into a more adventurous life in the Kingdom of God."

—**David Clayton,** Ethos Church, Nashville, Tennessee

"I've seen some tough situations, but few things are tougher than seeing a hungry child. Mark and his team at MANA have a track record of making a huge difference in this arena; and if we all make an effort to learn from them, we could have a lot fewer hungry children in the world."

—**Eric Greitens,** Navy SEAL, author of *Resilience, Time* magazine's 100 Most Influential Americans 2013

"I am so proud of what Mark and MANA are doing in my home state and my boyhood summer home of Fitzgerald. I hope you'll be as inspired as I have been after reading this book that we can each do something to fight and end world hunger."

—**Johnny Isakson,** United States senator, Georgia

"This book will challenge you, as Mark has challenged me over the last twenty years, to see that feeding the least of these is very near the heart of God."

—**Brett Biggs,** CFO, Walmart International

"Mark Moore has that rare creative genius that looks at things in a fresh, inspiring, and completely unexpected way. And, more importantly, he does more than just *look* at things. He *actually does something* about what he sees and makes us all want to pitch in. This book is for everyone. It will capture your imagination and your heart and you will never again look at what it means to be fed in the same way."

—**Eva Archer-Smith,** executive coach and speaker

"This book contains some shockingly Jesus-like ideas. I would suggest you read it at your own risk—for your eyes may be opened and you heart moved."

—**Randy Harris,** speaker, author, professor at Abilene Christian University

"I don't know of a more visionary, driven, compassionate person than Mark Moore. This is a book that has been written from the trenches, working to get food for hungry kids and worshipping a God who loves to feed them. I hope every Christian reads this book and will come to appreciate that, in the end, when we stand before Jesus, he's not going to ask us so much about what we believed, but about whom we fed."

—**Jonathan Storment**, preacher at Highland Church of Christ, Abilene, Texas, author of *How to Start a Riot*

NOURISH

NOURISH

A GOD WHO LOVES TO FEED US

MARK MOORE

NOURISH

A God Who Loves to Feed Us

ISBN 978-0-89112-331-6 | LCCN 2015012614

Printed in the United States of America

LIBRARY OF CONGRESS CATALOGING-IN-PUBLICATION DATA

Moore, Mark, 1966-

Nourish : a God who loves to feed us / Mark Moore.

pages cm

Includes bibliographical references and index.

ISBN 978-0-89112-331-6 (alk. paper)

1. Food in the Bible. I. Title.

BS680.F6S36 2015

220.8'6413--dc23

2015012614

Cover design by Thinkpen Design, LLC

Interior text design by Sandy Armstrong, Strong Design

Leafwood Publishers is an imprint of Abilene Christian University Press

ACU Box 29138, Abilene, Texas 79699

1-877-816-4455 | www.leafwoodpublishers.com

15 16 17 18 19 20 / 7 6 5 4 3 2 1

For my wife Marnie, who has nourished my heart,
soul, mind, and strength for nearly twenty-five years.
I'm still as thrilled to see you every new day
as I was on our first date.

CONTENTS

FOREWORD

Mark Moore and I share more than a first name: we both love God, coffee, food, basketball, writing, missions, and peanut butter. I like Mark because he's not embarrassed to admit that his love and worship of things on that list are sometimes (sadly) out of whack and in no particular order.

I'm excited about this book because for me it provides the context of a powerful story that crossed my path and my ministry. I'll need to tell you that story for this foreword to make much sense:

In the fall of 2008, I first met Mark huddled in a corner of Ebenezers, our D.C.-based coffee shop, nurturing a dream in his off moments from his job on nearby Capitol Hill. While we were neighbors and worked on the same street, I didn't know him, but in a way I recognized him because more than two years earlier when my friend and I launched Ebenezers, we laid hands on the walls and wrote prayers on the floors and prayed for every person who would walk through our doors—which included Mark.

The most memorable moment for me from our Ebenezers launch in 2006 was when one of our staff members specifically prayed that Ebenezers would be a *dream factory*. It was one of those moments when you almost open your eyes during prayer to see if it impacted everyone else the same way. It was a specific prayer, a prophetic prayer. For me, Mark's MANA dream is an example of how God can answer one prayer in a way that will affect millions of lives. Mark would later write this to me in an email:

> The dream of MANA began in many ways in the dream factory of Ebenezers Coffeehouse. Its great coffee and free Wi-Fi made for the perfect office. As that dream began to gel and I began to pull together resources and relationships to pursue the area, Ebenezers often became the meeting place. Meeting after meeting occurred there. Many were planned and scheduled, as in "meet me at Ebenezers at 2:00 P.M.," but many more happened by accident. Those meetings led to new ideas, new partnerships, new opportunities, and new relationships that eventually brought us to where we are today. We have now made enough RUTF to feed and save a million children.

I wrote Mark back and told him this was more than a good idea; it was a God-idea. And when you get a God-idea, you need to take it captive and, as Paul said, "make it obedient to Christ." He did that, even choosing the basement of Ebenezers for the MANA launch event on October 16, 2009 (World Food Day). Within a year of that kickoff event, they had built and launched a factory that now pumps out millions of packets of special fortified peanut butter. So the circle goes . . . from our dream factory at Ebenezers to a real factory in a Georgia peanut field! I love it when God answers prayers!

While this book is not about MANA, in *Nourish,* Mark helps us see that our God has been putting God-ideas in the heads of people like you and me for thousands of years. These ideas are unlimited thanks to the creative imagination of our Father, and whether they be about basketball, books, or factories, God is always seeking to nourish us and give us not only the energy to survive, but the creative energy to dream big. In *Nourish,* Mark starts in a garden, because that's where the God/Man story begins—with *a God who loves to feed us,* providing the very best to his sons and daughters. By the book's end, Mark reminds us that God shows up as a man and Satan's very first temptation of the living Christ is about food. Jesus in his ministry seems to always be headed to or coming from a meal. Finally, Jesus leaves his disciples with the charge, "Feed my sheep, feed my sheep, feed my sheep." Even if you've read Scripture your entire life, you'll be surprised as Mark reveals the obvious theme you somehow missed—that food, hunger, bread, and nourishment are everywhere.

As you read *Nourish,* resist the urge to focus on differentiating between so-called spiritual food and normal food, and just enjoy reading how our Father's purpose is to keep our whole beings nourished and healthy. Sit down with a cup of coffee and some peanut butter, and when you're done, I'm betting you'll be inspired with a few God-ideas of your own that could very well change a million lives—but will certainly change yours first.

Mark Batterson

INTRODUCTION

This book is not for everyone; only for people who eat.

Similarly, this book is not for all Christians; only for those who care about spiritual nourishment.

Just as no humans exist who do not eat (other than perhaps a small group of people who have decided not to go on living), even so we are not likely to find any spiritually alive people who do not nourish themselves with spiritual food.

Those of us who do eat, think about food and care about it a lot. Sometimes our food habits and hang-ups and obsessions occupy our thoughts, but usually the more mundane and never-ending utilitarian aspects of food occupy our minds. Or, more aptly put, we don't really have to think about what we're going to eat and when, because these concerns hang out in the back of our minds and rumble in our stomachs until they push their way to the top spot on our priority list. We call this process "hunger." It can be both wonderful and awful at the same time.

Our human fascination with food is not just about basic hunger. Our concerns about being nourished go far beyond that. Moms scramble to plan meals to keep fuel in kids' bodies. Or we indulge in a fun side of food when we are preparing feasts for family gatherings and social events where we can interact with those we love.

Dealing with food concerns can reveal all sorts of extremes in who we are and how we act. Indeed, how we deal with food may expose us when we are most generous or most stingy. Our handling of food may be regulated or spontaneous. Fancy or plain. Complicated or simple. Food may comfort us at one moment and torment us the next. It generates in us a gamut of emotions and reactions that few other things can unleash.

All of us occasionally get busy and forget to eat, but we have in us this *frenemy* called hunger who is always there to remind us that we missed a meal. Hunger is in fact both friend and foe. It starts with gentle prodding to get our attention and then, if ignored, ramps up to a shout so loud we can't pay attention to anything else. Hunger the friend is there to remind us that life must be nourished if we want to stay alive. Hunger the foe is there to kill us in the end if we persistently ignore its signals.

Such is food to the human—part fuel, part fun, part friend, part foe—and we often are unable to discern which role it is playing at any given time.

While we do not always manage it well, those of us who are believers think that God designed this system. As this book will argue, we serve a God who loves to feed us. Yet we have this tendency to fill ourselves with the wrong stuff. God wants us to be nourished, but far too often all of us choose to be malnourished. This is true both physically and spiritually. The apostle Paul is famous for confessing, "I don't do what I want to do." In few areas is this truer for all of us than in our relationship with food and eating. We fill ourselves with what we know is the wrong stuff, only to feel awful about it afterward. We misuse food. Sometimes we worship it. Then we look in a mirror and moan with Paul, "O wretched man that I am!"

Now being tested and tried by food is nothing new to humans, but what is new is the moment in exact time in which we have been graced to inhabit this planet called Earth. Had we been born eighty years ago, most of us would have been born on a farm and would be among a crowd who knew firsthand where food comes from. The apples you and I eat likely have been sitting in a fridge anywhere from six to eighteen months. That's just one example of how even the most traditional varieties of food we eat now come to us in ways that have become possible only in the last few years.

Fifty years ago each of us likely would have known a farmer in our family or in our inner circle of friends. Thirty years ago we would have had parents and grandparents who could tell us impassioned, firsthand accounts of where our food came from and how hard it was to grow and harvest. Today, you and I are among the first humans on this planet who really have no idea where our food comes from. If you doubt this, ask a kid, and he or she will respond with either Walmart or Whole Foods or the name of a nearby supermarket.

No wonder we have a resurgence of a "foodie" crowd—a generation of people dedicated to greater awareness of the food that goes into their bodies. Foodies love to eat, but they also want the story. They want to know who grew it, picked it, shipped it, and preserved it. This passion might be a bit faddish, but it's nothing new. In fact, it's very old, a throwback to simpler and healthier times.

This book will contend that God himself is a foodie of sorts. He certainly was when he came in the form of Jesus. If you want proof, check out the book of Luke and see if you can find a chapter where Jesus is not either coming from or headed to a meal. See if you can read a chapter without stumbling onto a story or a lesson or a crowd that does not have farming or food in it somewhere. Could it be that he was born in a manger, not for sentimental reasons, but because the God who loves to feed us was determined that we not miss the truth that he had shown up to feed and nourish an acutely malnourished and unhealthy world? Jesus hailed from Bethlehem, known as the House of Bread. And when the devil came to test our Lord, Satan himself started with hunger as his first strategy to derail Christ's mission.

Using the universal metaphor of eating and hunger to teach deep truths about spiritual nourishment, Christ one day told a group of people, "I am the bread of the world." On that same occasion he freaked out his Jewish food-rule-obsessed followers when he told them to eat his flesh and drink his blood (John 6). Most of them left when he said this.

"How can this man give us his flesh to eat?" the crowd carped.

"This is a hard teaching," his own disciples agreed. No doubt, for them it was.

To drive home the point, Jesus looked at his few remaining followers and asked, "What about you? Are you leaving, too?"

"Where else would we go?" Peter answered.

Jesus had plenty to say about both spiritual hunger and regular hunger, and he seemed to delight in tying the two together in ways that confused people.

The CDC tells us we are the first generation of Americans to have kids who will not live longer than we do, at least in part because of this widespread dysfunctional relationship with food. I hope the thoughts I share with you in the pages the follow will blur the lines and enable some of us to toggle back and forth between our struggles with physical food and spiritual food.

Some of my fellow evangelicals may feel that I stray when I talk about the physical too much. In my defense, I offer the words of George Bernard Shaw, who said, "I can't talk religion to a man with bodily hunger in his eyes." Those of us who have spent many a Sunday in church know that Shaw was right. Along about noon we quit listening, no matter how good the preacher is. The timely onset of hunger, mild as the case may be, renders the average human incapable of listening to even the most articulate and well-intended. Yet our response to others focused on physical hunger is often just what the disciples said to Jesus when they saw the crowds. "These people are hungry, Lord. *Send them away* so that they might feed themselves." Jesus replied, "You feed them." Physical feeding mattered to Jesus.

On the other hand, my secular friends will no doubt feel that I get too involved here with spiritual talk and Bible quoting. Please stay tuned, because I think this book will provide you plenty of ammo to counter your church friends' sincere but misguided tendencies to limit their outrage about moral issues in America to certain topics without ever considering the moral failure of the church to heed Jesus' continual and persistent call for them to feed the hungry.

My goal in this book is simple: I hope it will engage you with stories that keep you reading. When you are done, if someone asks you if the book was about spiritual hunger or physical hunger, I hope you will say, "I don't know. I couldn't tell." If this blurring of lines between the two is not even fuzzier than when you started, I will have failed.

I realize it is poor form for a writer to set out to confuse his audience, but I take some solace in the fact that Jesus seemed intent on doing this as well. It seems to me that he would be thrilled if we got the picture that the hole we feel inside us is there so that we might choose to be nourished by a God who loves to feed us.

Chapter One

IN THE BEGINNING—GOO VS. GOD

"Stay hungry. Stay foolish."

—**Steve Jobs**, Stanford Commencement Speech 2005

When God made us humans, we started in a garden, not for sentimental reasons but because our Creator God wanted us to be well nourished and to experience life at its fullest and best. We were tossed out of Eden because we humans chose malnutrition over nutrition. It was through food that Adam and Eve were initially tempted, and as a curse for the man's poor choices about food, the Creator told Adam that nourishing himself with food now would be much tougher in a regular garden. Soon his sons were fighting and killing over food and God issues, and so began a long saga that continues today—a God who loves to feed us, and a malnourished world.

That's the God-version as I know it, as Christian and Muslim and Jewish traditions have handed it down through the years. It sounds like an absurd story, a fairy tale, in these modern times. It sounds ridiculous and uneducated, in fact, until we listen to the "educated" version.

The goo-version of the story says man made a god. But before that, somehow rock came to be, and rocks collided and became stardust. As particle physicist Lawrence Krauss (a seriously smart guy, by the way) likes to say, "It's the most poetic thing I know. That we are literally all stardust. That the atoms that make up your left arm are not from the same planet or asteroid as the ones that make up your right arm."

The goo-version theorizes that after these primeval rocks collided, eventually there was goo. Somehow the goo grew opposable thumbs, stood upon two feet, and eventually turned into a man. Obviously I'm a theist, so I am certainly selling the goo-version short here, but not by a whole lot. The entire happening is unlikely and preposterous—just like our God-version. No higher ground seems to be offered here for smart people—just goo vs. God. The goo-view says we all got here by accident, and the God-view says we humans got here on purpose for a purpose.

Those two worldviews inform and divide our country, a divide that isn't getting any smaller. As Lawrence Krauss says, "Science never asks why, and when it does, it really means how."

But getting bogged down in the differences in those two is of less use than noticing the incredible similarities of the two. Whether we are here on purpose or by accident, whether we are goo-creatures or God-creatures, both stories (shall we call them faiths?) offer us a narrative that begins in a garden.

The earliest thing we know, categorically and with any historical certainty about humans, is that we really got our act together and formed something called "civilization" around a garden. It was in the Fertile Crescent, the land between the rivers, where the first men (and women) known to anthropologists managed for the first time to grow more food than they actually needed. We know this from our world history classes, and we know it with certainty because those early ancestors actually wrote it down and Leonard Woolley dug it up. Etched in clay tablets unearthed by Woolley and his team, who dug in Iraqi soil for twelve long, amazing years from 1922 to 1934, are accounting records that basically say things like, "Elki traded three bushels of corn to Ashkem for two vessels." These writings were found in and around Mesopotamian sites like the ancient city of Ur, home to the Sumerian peoples (in southern Iraq today). These ancient records are really pretty mundane as historical documents go, but they are anything but trivial, given that they are the earliest extant documents about the humans who preceded us.

Thomas Cahill in his great book *Gifts of the Jews* rightfully recognizes that thus begins what we call "history." Anything we claim to know about anything before that period is largely a guess. Cave paintings, reconstructed pots, bones, and carbon dating all give us a decent guess at what happened before that period. But that's all it is. Largely a guess. But here in the ancient writings of Sumer and Ur we have the first tangible human history. Real notes written by real people. Boring stuff like basic accounting. All of it, most of it anyway, revolved around their gardens: who grew what and who swapped it for what in the world's first complex economy. Here men and women first grew more than they needed, and thus it freed up a bunch of people to do things such as painting their huts or making pots. Metalworkers thrived, plows got better, gardens grew, and the Stone Age was gone for good. Combine all of this with a healthy dose of slave labor from less fortunate conquered neighbors, and we have what has come to be known as "progress."

So the God-people have their narratives of Adam and Eve and the goo-people have their historical artifacts. For the latter group, we are stardust infused with happenstance-accidental life. For the other, we are dust with life breathed into us by an intentional creative force for good. Believing either one may be guesswork, faith, or science, but both narratives basically begin in a garden.

Chapter Two

HUNGER: A HISTORY

"All of Upper Egypt was dying of hunger to such a degree that everyone had come to eating their children."

—Inscription from the Egyptian Tomb of Ankhtifi, 2000 BC

Either garden version above has humans gardening not so much because they liked it, but because they were in a constant scramble to fight off hunger. If you are human, hunger is your oldest and most persistent foe. Evidently, the garden thing failed from time to time, as it became a problem for the people of Ankhtifi's time, the land-between-the-rivers people, who lived more than two thousand years before Christ. I'm not an Egyptologist, but it seems safe to say that eating one's children qualifies as less than idyllic times. Scholars think this "eating their children" comment is not necessarily to be taken at face value, that it might be a bit of exaggeration to impress either the gods or inscription-readers-to-come—people like you and me. Inscriptions in the same tomb rave about Ankhtifi being "a near perfect ruler, feeding the hungry and bringing peace." Each line ends with "for such a man I am." That's hieroglyphic for "that's just how I roll." Exaggerated or not, the fact that Ankhtifi (who apparently put significant thought into his tomb inscriptions) found such a prominent place for the role of hunger is telling. People had plenty to be afraid of in those days, and hunger was apparently somewhere near the top of the list.

Perhaps more telling than ancient crypt inscriptions are the numbers we know from later history, where historical facts come together and find agreement with God- and goo-people alike. As record keeping and data improve, the evidence of hunger mounts and the numbers get bleaker: In 1347 two-thirds of Italy's population reportedly starved in the Great Famine. From 1845–50 the "great hunger" in Ireland claimed more than a million lives. During 1932–33 in Ukraine, hunger and famine killed about seven million people. In 1943–44 in Bengal and India, hunger brought death to four million more. Then in 1958–62 an estimated thirty million people died in China from the same serial killer—hunger. Disease might kill you quicker, but whatever hunger lacks in speed, it makes up for in tenacity. It has humbled and demoralized and bullied us puny humans for millennia. And while our scientific genius has made amazing progress against many diseases in modern times, our track record and the forecast for our battle with hunger still looks pretty bleak.

What's creepy is that while hunger can be deadly and daunting for sure, it's also something so common that every human awakens to it every single day. Since all of us feel it, we also have a unique ability either to empathize with or to dismiss people who struggle with it. Each of us has said it a hundred times—"I'm starving!" We say it when we aren't actually starving. We are just hungry. But with that hunger comes all sorts of emotions: grumpiness that may give way to outright anger, and, if hunger persists, anger gives way to an even more debilitating emotion—fear. So when we hear news reports of others who are hungry and we feel sympathy for them, we also tend to compare and wonder if this is the simple hunger we all meet every day or if it is the real killer. We see others in this predicament and we tend to think, at least to ourselves, "Oh, really? How hungry are you? Quantify it for me." Those are simple but tough queries, and the answer, to be accurate in English anyway, requires us to switch to another language. Words like *starving, malnourished,* and *anorexic* all are there to clarify and emphasize the severity of hunger when qualifiers like "very" don't seem to do the trick. And when we see people in these situations, the internal emotions of anger and fear too often give way to the final human emotion, a feeling of helplessness. We give up, and do nothing. We feel awful, then we turn the channel and watch the game.

Describing Hunger

As everyday, normal humans, we find it hard to set aside emotion and talk objectively about hunger. Scientists, if they are to do their jobs well, are called to be unemotional and exact, so they have developed a scientific explanation of hunger that clearly and sequentially enumerates its severity along a spectrum. They call it a disease or ailment, and as such it is listed in the International Classification of Diseases among ICD-9 codes. Google that term and pay particular attention to ICD-9 numbers 260–269, which cover the whole range of nutritional problems that affect humans from *under-* to *over-*nutrition. If you read that list, chances are you won't feel too bad when as a layperson you find yourself using descriptive terms like "sort of" and *"super"* in efforts to quantify and describe the various stages and severity of hunger. After all, who wants to say, "I am nearing ICD-9 code 261. Let's stop and get a pizza"? Or, "Those jeans make you look like you suffer from ICD-9 code 268"?

To his credit, Nobel prize-winning economist Amartya Sen opted for the simplest language at his disposal when, in his research on the economics of famine, he called the famine-induced part of this hunger range "regular starvation." The Food and Agriculture Organization of the United Nations (FAO) estimates that there are nearly a billion people suffering from "regular starvation," a condition they also call "undernourished" or "chronically hungry," depending on what point along the spectrum someone falls. These are fairly recent studies of a billion people! A billion, by the way, is a lot.

The fact that stats like this slip by us without completely shocking us and awakening us to some sort of immediate and urgent action is either odd or sad. We are either afraid of the ugly reality of worldwide hunger, in denial of its scope, or apathetic in regard to its impact. In my opinion, the goo-people are off the hook here. Not that they don't or shouldn't care (evidence is they do care more than we church people do), but they can at least credibly claim a Malthusian[1] premise that we have planet that can support only so many humans, and evolutionary reality will trim the herd to a sustainable level. God-people think, and have always thought, that's nonsense. We think that every human is here on purpose for a purpose and that our God is a God of abundance and not scarcity. Jesus apparently shared this view, because every time we turn around in the Gospels he is feeding a whole bunch of people in a way that his disciples seem to think is impossibly sustainable.

Hunger's New Face

Hunger's long history with humanity has traditionally been the same old story of starvation and deprivation. Lately, in some countries anyway, hunger seems to have cleverly figured out new ways to kill humans, just when humans figured they might have enough satellite-equipped tractors to have it whipped by ever-increasing food production. It turns out that humans with an overabundance of food overnourish themselves and tend to assuage their hunger with the wrong types and amounts of food. They hunger, or long to be filled with the wrong foods, so much so that, as I noted earlier, the richest country in the world has given birth to the first generation of little humans that will not, on average, live longer than their parents. Opportunistic maladies like heart disease and diabetes and extreme obesity shave years off our lives, almost as ruthlessly as starvation did in centuries past. Even in developing countries such as Kenya and Uganda, urban dwellers in the rising middle class are now more likely to face health issues related to obesity than to lack of food. It's all mal-nutrition. Once again the Latin prefix for "bad" turns out to be deadly accurate when applied in this case.

While obesity is a worthwhile topic for a book about hunger, it will not be the focus of this one. I mention it here simply to remind us that there is little difference between those of us who struggle with too much food and those who currently struggle with food shortages and hunger. In my job running MANA Nutrition, I often speak about malnutrition and how our product is used in the fight against it in its acute forms. In doing so, I invariably end up fielding questions from sympathetic audience members. One reoccurring question goes something like this: "Why are these people starving? Some of us grew up poor and on a farm, and times were tough, but we never starved. Are these people lazy? Are they uneducated? Are they bad farmers?" In almost every instance these questions are sincere and stem from a true desire to understand rather than to judge or blame.

The answer I always give is: "These people are just like you and me." They make good choices sometimes, and bad ones at other times. They have good luck sometimes and bad luck at other times. But in addition to good/bad choices and good/bad weather, they often live in a culture with some bad attitudes, assumptions, and habits around food. We (some of us) feed kids nothing but cheese puffs and sodas, and they get malnourished, or obese. They (some of them) feed kids nothing but millet and plantains, and they get malnourished. Why? Because there is a weird mixture of our cultures and our parents' habits and our priorities that seems to drag us into a situation where the only foods in the cupboard (and, sadly, the only foods our taste buds crave) are cheese puffs and sodas or the millet and plantains. Add extreme poverty to the mix and the fact that no safety nets exist in most developing countries, and a kid missing meals quickly spirals into a deadly, dramatic bout with the kind of hunger that we rarely see here in the United States.

Here at home in the United States at the time when I am writing this book, we have a first lady who has decided that the best way she can use the soap box afforded her is to get messages to our kids that might break this spiral started by our dysfunctional relationship with food. In many African countries a similar focus on nutrition has started to come from the top. Here we are scrounging for the resources to equip our health-care system to fund this sort of proactive attitude toward wellness. In developing countries the reactive dollars show up and get spent long before any proactive dollars are even considered. Nutrition is a proverbial step-child everywhere in health-care budgets. Our old enemy hunger knows this and loves it. Just like a lion on the hunt, hunger knows that the young ones are easiest to take down and kill. Disproportionately it is children who suffer and die. Severe malnutrition kills one more child roughly every nine seconds. As will be mentioned elsewhere in this book but is worth repeating, more kids are dying from hunger than from AIDS, malaria, and tuberculosis combined.

Whatever nomenclature we use, while few of us are experts in the field of nutrition, all of us are experts of a sort when it comes to hunger. We come face to face with hunger every day in our lives, so we know it well. Most of us who have time to sit and read a book like this one are not facing the sort of hunger that can kill, but just missing a meal reminds us how awful it must be to try to survive in that spot. Given our expertise and insider knowledge about hunger, we are therefore uniquely qualified on one hand and responsible on the other to help our fellow-hunger sufferers.

Where do we start? As Dr. Milton Tectonidis of Doctors Without Borders suggests, maybe we should ask ourselves, "Where are [children] wasted? Where are they dying?" Their Nobel Prize-winning work on this subject suggests that the first six years in a child's life are a window of opportunity. If we hit that window with proper nutrition, kids can grow and develop and go on to a good life. If we miss that window, it's too late. It's as simple as that.

The ICD-9 codes tell us there is a whole range of malnutrition, and addressing that entire range is a complex undertaking. The reasons people end up in those ranges are varied and complex. So are the problems they face. Children starve today because of famines, drought, bad agriculture, politics, bad luck, war, cultural eating habits, and disease. These and other factors pile up and work in conjunction with one another, making noble efforts to "end hunger" seem like something of a fool's errand. Indeed, we may never eradicate or eliminate the entire 260–269 range, but it is at least feasible to think that we could, through a great, global, coordinated effort, empower mothers to put a stop to the plague of babies that die every day simply because they lack the most basic food. In other words, the little sliver of kids at the end of the pie chart that die from Severe Acute Malnutrition can be quantified, addressed, and stopped. How much of it do we want to stop? All of it. In fact, Isaiah 65:20 gives us this kind of vision for the kingdom of God. "Never again will there be in it an infant that lives for but a few days" (NIV).

If we serve a God who loves to feed us, then we must assume that this entire chapter about rampant hunger on our globe describes a calamity that does not fit into his ideal plan of abundance. If we are to attempt to understand where we are going, we must first look at where we have been. Indeed, not just where we have been lately, but where we started. Those of us who ascribe to Abrahamic faiths think we started in a garden.

Note

[1]Thomas Malthus (1766–1834), English economist and clergyman. In *An Essay on the Principle of Population* (1798) he argued that without the practice of "moral restraint," the population tends to increase at a greater rate than its means of subsistence, resulting in the population checks of war, famine, and epidemic.

Chapter Three

THE GARDEN

"My weaknesses have always been food and men—in that order."

—Dolly Parton

The creation story has us in a garden, not for sentimental reasons, but because that's the logical place a God who wanted to feed people would place them. Humans are not like God; he needs nothing outside himself to sustain himself. So, for the humans in the Garden, the very act of eating is an act of dependence. He made them (us) from dirt, breathed his Spirit into them, and made it so that this amazing, magical, otherwise inexplicable thing we have in us called life had to be recharged, reenergized, and "kept alive" through ongoing external energy sources provided by the God who feeds us.

As we know, in the middle of that amazing, lush, life-giving Garden was a tree, put there by God for reasons we cannot fully know but can only guess. I have yet to read a fully compelling reason as to why, but the best I know is that the freewill option that comes as part of the gift of life meant that God would allow these creatures of his to compete with him and his authority. They would not be robots or puppets. They would know love and choice, and this meant the ability to choose a source of energy that he knew would not sustain them. I don't necessarily like that explanation, but I am writing and typing and thinking here while using borrowed life and energy from God, and it's the best my limited brain can do.

As we know, in the Garden near this tree, Eve encountered the king of malnutrition, the life-taker. "You should eat this fruit that God does not want you to eat," the cunning serpent advised her.

"If I do that, I will surely die," Eve replied, being faithful to the Life-giver's warning about the sustainability of life.

The serpent's lie sounded something like this: "You won't die. That's a fairy tale. God is just selfish. He's hoarding the good stuff for himself. Oh, sure he's acting like he's the God who loves to feed you, but that's a crock. Why else would he forbid you to eat the very best-looking fruit? You want real life? Eat this stuff!"

The text says that the fruit was "pleasing to the eye," so she ate it. It's worth noting here that while every human must eat, not every human sees food in the same way. Ruby Payne, author of *A Framework for Understanding Poverty* and *Bridges Out of Poverty,* talks about the differences in the way the three basic socioeconomic classes see food. The poor see food and ask, "Is it enough?" The middle class look at food and ask, "Is it tasty?" The wealthy class ask, "Is it pretty?" The three groups view food through the lenses of supply, flavor, and presentation.

Note that Eve is exorbitantly rich, so she sees the fruit as a rich person does today. It looked pretty, the presentation was fabulous, and in a world where there was plenty to eat and where everything tasted great, this tipped the scales. Here we see that God is the original beautifier of everything, even food, so Eve's attraction to the beautiful food is not bad. But her desire to nourish her body and soul with stuff not approved by God got her into a pickle.

Ironically, all these centuries and millennia later we have not changed much or really come very far in our attitudes about food. Perhaps that's okay; perhaps these three ways of viewing food are actually gifts of God, each appropriate and healthy in its own right. But when they get out of whack, these attitudes malnourish both our bodies and our souls. Eve learned this the hard way, and we are still learning those lessons today.

Today about one out of every three people on our earth looks at food and asks, "Is there enough?" Some children see food only once a day, and far too many die every day from complications that arise from a basic lack of it. Even here in our country, the richest in the history of the world, as many as one in eight children go to bed hungry. Few, if any, actually starve to death, but you don't have to die to have food insecurity ruin your life and limit your future. Hungry kids can't focus on schoolwork. They drop out earlier and end up stuck on a path to poverty. Moreover, poor people are often served food that is highly processed, mass-produced, inexpensive, and immediately accessible. Many poor citizens in the United States, therefore, are obese, as fast food and open-and-serve foods are what they purchase and what they receive through distributions. We don't often recognize it as such, but this is actually a form of mal-nutrition. It is a misadjusted, improper relationship with food that causes disease, limits futures, and even, we are learning, diminishes mental capacity in the young.

Those of us in the middle class seldom obsess about presentation and how pretty our food is. Free from scarcity and unconcerned about presentation, we turn our food-focus to taste. The bad news for us is that sugar tastes great, and our demands for great taste have landed it in some form in almost everything we eat. Eat a regular non-whole-grain bagel and within about twenty minutes it will be sitting in your stomach with no discernible difference (to your gut and body) than if you had chosen to eat a bag of Skittles instead. Sugar in excess happens to be like rat poison for humans, and I say this, not as a foodie health nut, but as a rat who loves sugar poison more than almost anyone I know! So this normal, healthy, "does it taste good?" question is now masked by palates that only like the taste of stuff that really isn't very good for us. That's a problem if you care about life, because this generation's lives are being shortened. This truncated life span is due almost solely to our choices around food and nutrition. "You won't surely die!" said the serpent. "Eat it!"

Eve's fall to the "isn't it pretty?" temptation wasn't any worse than the other two food questions, but it landed her in a world of trouble nutritionally. Suddenly she found herself with her eyes opened to some new facts about food and how to feed herself—and therefore to some new facts about life. From now on, gardening would be a lot tougher for Adam and Eve. Now they would spend long days fighting weeds and offering up sweat and hard work to scratch out what we have come to call today "a living." Having kids (passing on the life-gift) would be a pain, and feeding them would be a pain.

Before long the curse was all too real, because the kids started fighting over food/God issues, and the worst possible thing happened. One son killed the other. Abel obeyed God and offered food from his flock; Cain brought food from the ground. Their attempts to nourish themselves had led to death. It is interesting that this is the first time we see human death in Scripture, and it comes wrapped in a story about food and poor choices. The fingerprints of Satan the life-taker are all over this story. All these years later we remain malnourished, but we are not without hope. Supply, flavor, and presentation—Scripture continually points to a God who seeks to bless us with all three. Most importantly, we find plenty of hints in the Gospels that Jesus actively promoted all three, especially the first two.

Indeed, Scripture begins in a garden and ends in a garden, begins with a lyric of abundance and ends with a feast. In between is a long journey, but we must not miss the continual theme of a generous God who loves to feed us.

Chapter Four

OUT OF UR AND INTO NOT KNOWING WHERE WE ARE GOING

"Business is business and business must grow, regardless of crummies in tummies, you know."

—**Dr. Seuss**, *The Lorax*

In Chapter Two, I mentioned Sir Leonard Woolley's work in the 1920s, work that is significant to the goo-people and the God-people alike. The God-people know of Ur because their very first archetypal hero hailed from there. His name was Abraham, and the Bible says he left Ur "not knowing where he was going," because he was called by God to start something altogether new. Many a preacher, imam, and rabbi has made hay from this tale. And that's interesting, since having your eighty-year-old leader hear voices and get lost in the desert is hardly a flattering founding narrative.

When Abraham became the first member of his clan to hear the voice of this new God and promptly wandered out of town with his barren wife, he must have walked within sight of that ziggurat that Leonard Woolley dug up centuries later. Now fully excavated, it is impossible to miss today, even with a good chunk of its top missing. In Abraham's day it would have been abuzz with activity and towering into the heavens. The ziggurat was a piece in a temple complex that served as an administrative center for the city. It was a shrine of the moon god Nanna, the patron deity of Ur.

That impressive structure had been the brainchild of King Ur-Nammu, who dedicated it in honor of the god Nanna/Sîn, in approximately the twenty-first century BC during the Third Dynasty of Ur. It was actually finished later in that century by King Shulgi, who, in order to win the allegiance of the cities, proclaimed himself a god. Those of us who still find our identity wrapped up in Abraham's account can find some comfort in the fact that, as crazy as our story sounds to modern ears, at least our citizen of Ur did not imagine himself to be a god. Moreover, it seems that if he made up his story, he was determined to make up stuff that made his life wildly inconvenient at best.

As for King/god Shulgi, during his forty-eight-year reign he did not do too badly. Under his rule the city of Ur grew to be a thriving metropolis and the capital of a state that controlled much of Mesopotamia. It was New York City, Silicon Valley, and Washington, D.C., all rolled into one. It was the ultra-hip epicenter of the civilized world. And Abraham heard a voice that told him to reject all-things-Ur and wander out into the wilderness.

Perhaps the creepiest thing of all to our modern senses is the fact that human sacrifice took place around that ziggurat and temple area. The Sumerians fed their god in exchange for her feeding them. The Sumerian calendar was cyclical; it went with the crops. So they fed their moon god and, tit-for-tat, she fed them with blessings of harvests and food. Accordingly, slaves and other unfortunate humans were selected to be ritually killed and "fed" to their goddess.

So, while our kids' Zondervan Study Bibles omit the unsettling story of a dad raising a knife to kill his son, such a command from a god would likely not have seemed all that odd to Abraham. Surely he felt some irony and sadness in the realization that the God who chose to speak to him asked for the blood of his son, and not for that of slaves or enemies. We all know the story. Abraham complied with the voice in his head, but God stopped his arm and said in effect, "I am not that sort of god. You don't feed me. I feed you."

If we raise our eyes from the land between the rivers and look across the millennia, we see that all of history is full of examples of people who tried to feed their god. Today, as temperatures rise and the glacier retreats from Machu Picchu, we find more and more perfectly preserved examples of child sacrifice. We now know with more certainty than ever that human sacrifice was common in Aztec and Mayan culture. Their ziggurats, completely disconnected but oddly similar to those in Mesopotamia, had similar purposes. They were temples that in many cases fed their god. Ancient Greek and Roman paintings and pottery depict feasts prepared for the gods. Norse and Celtic traditions are full of god-feeding efforts as well. Everywhere we look, throughout the ages and cultures, the similarities are shocking. *People seem to feel a need to feed god.*

And so it would be for the "new" God of Abraham. The Semitic desert nomads whom history would come to know as the Jews would have their own obsessions with God-feeding and sacrifice. Throughout it all, though, their historians noted messages from YHWH, the God so powerful they dared not pronounce or even write his name. These messages had this God repeatedly saying, "Let me remind you again. You don't feed me." We'll get to those instances in the next chapter, but for now it's enough to note that with Abraham a new epic has begun. Or at least that seems to be the intent of this new God, if he can get people to listen.

With all respect to Mr. Woolley and his archeological team, Abraham's departure is the most important happening to occur in and around Ur of the Chaldeans at that time in history. This is, indeed, one of the turning points in human history. For the God who loves to feed us enters the scene to distance himself from the other gods of the day. He yanks Abraham out of the hippest, coolest, most advanced place in the world and brings him to the middle of nowhere to teach him a lesson. "I feed you," he tells him. And while Abraham is the first to hear this, as we will see in the characters this God chases and feeds in the future, he won't be the last.

Chapter Five

FROM SOUP TO (COMPLETELY) NUTS!

"He was a bold man that first ate an oyster."

—Jonathan Swift

As Abraham follows the God who loves to feed him, he is spared the gruesome task of feeding his son to God. God stops his hand and "provides" a ram for the sacrifice. For Christians this is a powerful foreshadowing of a God who would refuse to allow us to sacrifice our sons to him, but amazingly later sacrifices his own for us. It strikes a chord with all humanity, because deep down we see the truth that freedom is never free; it comes from the blood of our sons and daughters. Don't mistake this as sappy patriotism that glorifies war (there does seem to be this odd, sad, cross-cultural, and panhistorical equation that blood plus sons [and now daughters] equals freedom). If I were to toss my Christian hat aside, I might say that the gods of freedom seem to want to drink blood before they share freedom with mere humans. Abraham's risky venture starts off with a bold move in Genesis 12 but, unfortunately for Abraham, verse 10 of that chapter takes us back to the theme of food and the lack thereof. "Now there was a famine in the land," we are told. "So Abram went down to Egypt to reside there as an alien, for the famine was severe in the land" (Gen. 12:10 RSV).

Eventually his son Isaac grows up and before long we see that he has a couple of sons named Jacob and Esau. The most famous story we know about them is a food/hunger story. Like Cain and Abel before them, they have sibling rivalry issues and could have used some counseling to acquire anger management and conflict resolution skills. But those of us who have brothers know that brothers fight, and, but for God's grace, the local sheriff, and strict mothers, we might well have killed our brothers a time or two along the way. The good guy in this story is a complete scoundrel for ripping off his brother the way he did. The bad guy is an idiot for selling his birthright for soup. We see a little of ourselves in both of them—the scoundrel and the shortsighted idiot—one or the other too often present in our own mismanagement of our lives. The God who loved to feed them both must have been saddened by this, his children cheating, hoarding, manipulating over food and hunger. We Jews and Christians are, if I may borrow from Seinfeld, all descendants of a soup salesman far more manipulative and scary than the guy he called his Soup Nazi.

Jacob the soup guy has a few kids of his own—a dozen, to be exact. The God who loves to feed him changes his name to "Israel," and this pack of scoundrel-sons seems to be no better than their DNA had produced in the past. They grow jealous of the youngest of the crew because he has bolder dreams than they and, because Daddy loves his mother more than theirs, this prodigy has emerged as their father's favorite. So they decide to do away with him. They are well on their way to doing it until one with a conscience (if you can call it that) decides that selling him into slavery would be more profitable than killing him. So they swipe his coat and toss him into a pit, and Joseph ends up back with the land-between-the-rivers people as a slave. The expensive coat, now all bloodied up, goes back to their father, a mute message that the dreamer-boy has become food for some wild animal. Surely, as any parent who loses a child, Jacob must have questioned why the God who supposedly loves to feed his family would allow such a tragedy. After much suffering, the heartbroken father would later learn there was more to the story.

It's a very long story, well worth reading in Genesis 37–50, but the short version of that Joseph story is that Joseph's trip to the pit was about much more than his brothers being jerks. It was nothing less than God's plan to feed the world and save his people from widespread famine. Joseph's dream about food and sheaves of grain bowing down was a direct message from God about the role he would play and the role the land-between-the-rivers people (not far from Ur) would play with their fertile land and their amazing farming technology. What we learned from Leonard Woolley and Sumer is that these land-between-the-rivers people were crazy-good at growing food. By Joseph's time, several centuries after the times uncovered by Woolley, they have all but perfected their agricultural art. Joseph's gift of being a dreamer, while rejected by "God's people, the sons of Israel," is embraced by Pharaoh, who like ancient King Shulgi (ancient to Pharaoh anyway) thinks he is a god himself. How interesting it is that an arrogant leader with a literal god-complex is more open than the very people God was plotting to feed, but that's a long sermon for another day. The point is that the God who loves to feed us is hard at work, manipulating circumstances and directing even those who arrogantly think they are his god-equal. I've glossed over the Joseph story here, but it's worth a closer look. We'll do that in Chapter Six and see how Joseph both sold out and bought into the grand narrative of a God who loves to feed us.

Chapter Six

The Dreamer

"I have the audacity to believe that people everywhere can have three meals a day for their bodies, education and culture for the minds, and dignity, equality and freedom for their spirits."

—Martin Luther King Jr

I am, no doubt, a dreamer. Ask my wife, my friends, anyone who knows me, and they'll tell you a dozen stories about half-cocked, unfinished ideas I had that got about one-third done and lost momentum (for years this book was one of those unrealized dreams). Interspersed between all the stalled and unfinished dreams are the occasional dreams I launch that actually make it.

We say we like dreamers in America, but we are skeptical, to say the least. There is a story that I think puts the Joseph we meet in the Bible into perspective. Bear with me for a second as I tell it.

Bob Lutz in his book *Car Guys vs. Bean Counters* does a great job articulating how the dreamer-visionary guys and gals need execution-focused partners to get anything done. Conversely, he argues that any company left only to the bean counters is doomed as well. Dreamers like to look forward and imagine what's coming; bean counters look back and bet that their ledgers tracking past performance are better indicators of the future than silly, hopeful dreams.

Lutz argues that bean counters and their refusal to engage or listen to the dreamers is what killed General Motors. In Lutz's nomenclature, the "bean counters" took over and GM never made another truly cool car until they eventually dissolved into bankruptcy and reemerged. In fact, Lutz tells us, once the bean counters took full control of GM (a well-intended move, since GM was tanking in the '70s) GM completely disposed of the "car guys" and no one ever asked the fundamental question, "I wonder if we could make a really cool car?" Instead, they moved on to a business equation that goes sort of like this:

> *Beginning Situation:* I have a pile of money.
> *End Goal:* I want to have a bigger pile of money.
> *In-between Time:* The money has to temporarily take the form of a car, until someone gives us money for it and we have a bigger pile of money.

I found Lutz's simple, elegant articulation of this sort of business mentality to be profound. Who cares about cool cars? In fact, that whole interim time when the money unfortunately has to be a car is really just a big headache.

As a product of Flint, Michigan, myself, proudly born and raised in that blue-collar mecca, I watched it all unfold firsthand.

I am also an Apple guy, a geeky sort, who has been loyally buying their products since the late 1980s when I was in college. The movie *Jobs* portrays Apple founder Steve Jobs as a visionary-dreamer type, with a head full of ideas but very little practicality. Eventually, the bean counters run Jobs out, citing his refusal to consider costs as the reason for their demise. While the movie hardly portrays Jobs as a good guy or as a smart businessman, it shows (true or not) how Apple wallowed in mediocrity and failure until Jobs came back and restored the dreams and the visions.

What happened to Jobs and to the 1970s execs at GM is exactly what happened to Joseph in the Bible story. Joseph was a dreamer! What happens to dreamers? They get tossed into pits by people who get tired of their impractical and sometimes self-aggrandizing, arrogant dreams. Moreover, following Bob Lutz's observations, dreamers need a bean-counter teammate to execute and get things done. One might argue that Joseph in this story literally becomes history's first recorded bean counter as he plans and sacks away beans and grains for a time of need. Or maybe it's more accurate to say that the dreamer Joseph now has a powerful, bean-counter teammate in Pharaoh, and the two of them set out to take over the world in a giant game of Monopoly.

While the dreamer part of Joseph's story is rather easy for us to recognize and takes on a major role in our retelling of the story, modern readers tend to miss what is perhaps the main part of the story. Joseph didn't really have dreams so much as God did. God had a plan to save the world from famine. This particular famine was catastrophic, and in Scripture it's unclear to what extent God caused it or allowed it to happen. It is clear that the nation that had risen to be the best in the world at food production was where God wanted Joseph to be. The Egyptians, who had harnessed the Nile in the same way the land-between-the-rivers guys referred to in earlier chapters had harnessed the Tigris and Euphrates, now held out the only hope for that part of the world. Certainly they were positioned to do something that God's people, a wandering group of desert nomads, could not pull off. Pharaoh had a dream about what was to come, but he couldn't figure out what it meant. The explanation of that dream came from a foreigner, the longtime dreamer Joseph. Before long, as we know, Joseph the dreamer saw his dreams from earlier in life come true as well.

While it is often missed by Christians today, one can find a lot of similarities between Joseph and Jesus. If Jesus had a last name, it was, in fact, bar Joseph—son of Joseph. While both Joseph and Jesus were common names, I wonder if an early follower who had accepted Jesus as the long-awaited, though unorthodox, Jewish Messiah would have quickly seen the similarities in the two.

- Both chosen
- Both dreamed big
- Both sold
- Both shared their anointing
- Both betrayed
- Both arrested
- Both placed in a grave
- Both emerged from their pit
- Both wept
- Both revealed themselves to their betrayers
- Both saved God's people

The flannel-graph Joseph I grew up with in Sunday school classes was a definite good guy, placed there by God with perfect timing and planning. While Scripture makes it clear Joseph is a good guy—a literal savior—he is also one of the few Old Testament heroes void of a black mark or two. Moses, David, Jonah—the Jews were unique in history for writing well-rounded accounts of their leaders as both saints and scallywags. The Joseph we learn of is a saint of a guy, and whatever warts and character flaws he had as a normal human being are omitted from the Bible narrative.

But as Walter Brueggemann points out in his essay "The Myth of Scarcity," there are some troubling aspects to Joseph's role that we may not want to attribute to a God who loves to feed us. Joseph does save his people, but he also, by (unwittingly?) joining the pharaonic monopoly, acts in ways that eventually enslave his people. Pharaoh is determined to address this famine through centralized planning (not by depending on God, since Pharaoh thought himself a god), so he selects Joseph as the head of the planning commission. Caught between his people and his new king, Joseph sides with Pharaoh. As Brueggemann puts it, "How could he not! Pharaoh is so clever, and he understands the bureaucratic deployment of technology."

Survival for the Egyptians comes at a high price. They are not captured and forced into indebtedness; rather, they slowly, painfully, over a course of time, trade autonomy for food and dependency. It is not a sudden, brutal event that lands them in slavery, but a transaction in which they literally *sell* everything they have. Little by little, caught in a bad spot and desperately in need of the next meal, they sell their cattle, their wealth, and their land; and eventually, when they have nothing left to sell, they are left in a relationship that leads to the enslavement of future generations.

In Genesis 47, the people of Egypt come to Joseph looking for food. He not only has plenty, he has the *only* food. Joseph gives them food and takes their money. Scripture tells us this was a serious famine, and soon the people were back, once again looking for food. When all of the people ran out of cash, Joseph accepted as payment their means of production: donkeys, flocks, herds. He cleaned them out, horse by horse. The third year they are back at his feet groveling for food, this time bereft of money or livestock. They beg him: "Why should we perish before your eyes—we and our land as well? Buy us and our land in exchange for food, and we with our land will be in bondage to Pharaoh. Give us seed so that we may live and not die, and that the land may not become desolate"

(Gen. 47:19). With nothing left to sell, they sold themselves into his service. They were so desperate that they actually begged to become debt-slaves to the state. While bankruptcy today is certainly no fun, in those days it meant membership in a group that would forever be a year behind. As such, they would now perpetually work to pay off old bills, and with such a credit score, that would be a life sentence. As noted earlier, but often missed by modern debt-ridden readers, this form of slavery begins not with a violent abduction, but as an economic transaction.

Genesis 47:27 tells us that this debt-slavery to the state did not start off too badly for the people of Israel. They had possessions, they were fruitful and multiplied. Perhaps their reasoning was correct. As will be noted later, a time is coming when Joseph will not be around to pull strings, return their money, and ensure their fair treatment.

The powerful thing about this story is that most of us have been on both sides. When we reflect on our times as the hoarder, the bitter person, the wronged one, we may find either pleasure in the demise of those who have done us wrong or perhaps apathy toward their suffering, as we think to ourselves, "Serves you right. You got your just deserts." But we also see ourselves in the indentured Egyptians; slaves, not so much because we were captured or conquered in a single event, but because we came back and slowly sold ourselves little by little, until we woke up one day so deeply in debt that we couldn't catch up. This slavery to debt is an epidemic in our culture. It is the way of Pharaoh, and it has a way of turning each one of us into little hoarders like him.

The flannel-graph Joseph we know well was forgiving and gracious to his brothers, but perhaps he took a while to break through the bitterness of being tossed into a pit and sold off by his brothers. In Genesis it's just a few chapters, but in reality he had years to think it through, years to plan the next meeting. Perhaps Brueggemann is right and Pharaoh's intent was to spread his monopoly. Perhaps Joseph's motives were to help his brothers, teach them a lesson or two along the way, and save their skins in the end. Whatever the case, we see that he finally broke down and wept at the gravity of it all. He saw that God had a hand in this from the beginning. He saw that he had been an instrument in the hands of a God who loves to feed us.

Chapter Seven

A GAME OF MONOPOLY AND THE MYTH OF SCARCITY

"If more of us valued food and cheer and song above hoarded gold, it would be a merrier world."

—J. R. R. Tolkien

Occasionally as a family we will break out the game board on the kitchen table and engage in a long and intense game of Monopoly. These family fun times often end up troubling my wife Marnie as she sees her sons spiral into a ruthless competition where they gain increasing pleasure at the misfortune of their brothers. Brother against brother, as the game drags on, bad luck for one is pure joy for another. Begging and pleading can be heard from the one with the bad roll, while the one with the upper hand happily extends egregious terms for valuable property—or just wipes out his brother altogether. Such are the rules of Monopoly: the ruthless win and the unlucky or poor planners get crushed. Welcome to family game night in America!

We love the *game* Monopoly because it's fantasy. It allows us to playact something we have banished in real life. After we saw firsthand the evils that come from a monopoly, we outlawed it in business and relegated it to the realm of imaginary games. We formed laws against a commercial monopoly, laws that we still call on to keep it from creeping back into the modern marketplace. Yet a part of us (of me anyway) still respects and even idolizes the robber barons who ran the railroad and steel industries and "built" America. In the previous chapter I may have smacked of sacrilege as I questioned Joseph's motives. If you felt this while reading it, I felt it when I was writing it, because we American Christians tend to love the Joseph story. He personifies one of our highest values (albeit a quickly fading one) of planning ahead and saving. No doubt Joseph planned and saved, but for his boss, it seems the end goal was not the prudent and admirable virtue of saving for hard times, but the desire to control, manipulate, enslave, and hoard. Pharaoh's end game was to perpetuate the lie that he was in charge and was actually god. Pharaoh's worldview said, "Scarcity is upon us! There is not enough to go around! There will be winners and losers, and I will be a winner at the expense of others."

As mentioned earlier, Walter Brueggemann has an eloquent essay he calls "The Myth of Scarcity." In fact, in addition to reading my thoughts here, which were influenced by his reflections on scarcity, I'd encourage you to put down this book and Google search "Brueggemann Myth of Scarcity," and read his short essay. While Bruggemann's take on the Joseph Pharaoh story isn't gospel and has some shortcomings for sure, it's challenging to consider his view in light of our own culture.

If scarcity is indeed a myth, as Brueggemann's title suggests, then it has some serious implications. Nothing major really—only the very foundations of capitalism and our entire economy as we know it. Ha! Think about it. Stuff that we have a lot of is not worth much. Stuff that we don't have much of is worth a lot. There's only so much to go around, and that means there will be *haves* and *have-nots*. Brueggemann is crazy! Scarcity is actually common sense. Or is it?

Scarcity is the fundamental economic problem of having seemingly unlimited wants and needs in a world of limited resources. This is Economics 101 today, thanks to the work of British economist Lionel Robbins, who enshrined the notion when he penned his now classic definition of economics in his 1932 essay on the nature and significance of economic science. He offered the basic definition of economics that stuck: "the science which studies human behavior as a relationship between ends and scarce means which have alternative uses." It may seem simple, but Robbins was so brilliant and his contributions so important that the library at the London School of Economics (LSE) now bears his name, testimony to how his leadership there coincided with the ascendancy of LSE to the top rung of the academic ladder—at least the one that leads to the tip-top of the world of smart people and economics.

Indeed, Robbins seems to be right in defining our problem. Scarcity is a reality. Had we been listening, all of us would have learned that in eighth-grade economics. Gold is valuable because there's not that much of it. Not in comparison to other rocks anyway. Rare stuff has value, ubiquitous stuff has none. This isn't news, but the human family is still learning and relearning tough lessons about limited resources all the time. And while wasting resources once thought plentiful may never have been smart, such practices are certainly no longer acceptable. We have long been reminded of the scarcity of oil, and more recently the scarcity of water has been at the forefront of our minds. Perhaps the scariest of all scarcity issues, however, is food, where Malthusian projections of calamity have long loomed with concerns of an overpopulated planet that can't feed itself.

Robbins's 1932 definition of economics came just in time for much of the world to spend the next half a century ignoring its implications. With Americans leading the way, wealthy nations engaged in a form of wasteful, conspicuous consumption that burned up and squandered resources at a rate we now realize may have overheated our entire planet. Driven by scarcity, today we are starting to right our wasteful ship, with much still to learn and plenty of room for a more sensible approach to our collective use of everything from oil, to water, to food . . . to even air, if you live in Beijing.

Yet just as the pendulum had swung too far toward plenty, if we are not careful, it could swing us just as far out of whack toward scarcity. While a healthy view of scarcity may be good, it can also be a tool in the hands of hand-wringers who like to tout it in mythological proportions. Oil was supposed to run out in the late 1880s, then again in the 1920s, then in the '50s, and again in the '70s, but we seem to keep finding more. Water is increasingly in short supply in places where humans have settled over the last half century, yet basic science tells us that, other than minuscule amounts from random meteors, we have basically the same amount of water molecules present as the dinosaurs drank. (Granted, we keep settling in places that don't have enough water to go around.)

So, while scarcity is a hard truth, it's an odd truth in that it can, at times, be easily twisted into a myth. At least, that's what Frances Moore Lappé and Joseph Collins argued in their landmark 1977 book, *Food First: Beyond the Myth of Scarcity.* The narrative of hungry people on a planet that cannot sustain them is not true, Lappé and Collins insisted. Nearly ten years later, in 1986, along with Peter Rosset, they penned another classic, *World Hunger: 12 Myths,* in which they demonstrated convincingly that more than enough food was being produced in the world. The ensuing twenty-five years have been kind to their theories. World agriculture produces 17 percent more calories per person today than it did when they wrote *World Hunger,* despite a 70 percent population increase. According to the Institute for Food and Development Policy, the world today produces enough grain alone to provide every human being on the planet with 3,500 calories a day. In the book, they offer the following insight:

> That's enough to make most people fat! And this estimate does not even count many other commonly eaten foods—vegetables, beans, nuts, root crops, fruits, grass-fed meats, and fish. In fact, if all foods are considered together, enough is available to provide at least 4.3 pounds of food per person a day. That includes two and half pounds of grain, beans and nuts, about a pound of fruits and vegetables, and nearly another pound of meat, milk and eggs.[1]

If you are like me, this will sound to you like shockingly good news. Let's be clear. Hunger is no myth. The growling stomachs that torture millions of the world's children are not mythical or imagined. They are excruciatingly real. The myth here is the assertion that we do not have the ability and the resources to do something about it. When I set aside my view that the church is the primary way to engage and change the world, I actually think we have some good news in the government. This good news is that the most powerful country in the world is also the most generous in world history. The country that offered the Marshall Plan to the conquered rather than the historical boot on the neck remains as generous as ever. So while the right-headed scientists in the various fields of hydrology, petroleum engineering, and nutrition all warn us about the hard truth of scarcity, and in all of these areas demand that we curb our wasteful ways, the people of the United States through our government have not thrown up our hands in despair. We are helping feed our brothers and sisters in other countries with a paltry but impactful allotment of less than one percent of our budget. Our government is doing this because, for the most part, the church has decided it's not our job. One percent is nothing to brag about, but let's confess that it is more than most churches spend on feeding hungry people. Apparently we do better with our involuntary tax dollars than we do with our voluntary, charitable God-dollars.

The food aid and church conversations are for later, but let's close this chapter by getting back to the main point about scarcity. First, I argued that Brueggemann (and Lappé and Collins before him) had it right when they declared scarcity a myth. Then I argued the opposite and noted that what we might call the "law of scarcity" seems to be an undeniable force at work in our world. Confused? All I can say is that, as Jesus followers, we should expect this upside-down worldview. "Be first," the world says. "Be last," Jesus responds. "Aspire to have servants," the world advises. "Be a servant," Jesus teaches us. "There is not enough," the myth of scarcity would tell us. "There is plenty," responds the God of plenty.

Somehow, by the end of the Bible's first book, something has gone terribly wrong, and the myth of scarcity has won the day. The people of God are a far cry from where they started. The book of Genesis starts with abundance in a garden and ends with God's people coping with the scarcity of worldwide famine. Something had to give, and the God who loved to feed them had a plan. That's what the second book of the Bible is about. It's about God's people seeking a land flowing with milk and honey on a very long journey with a God who loves to feed them.

Note

[1]Frances Moore Lappé, Joseph Collins, and Peter Rosset with Luis Esparza, *World Hunger: 12 Myths* (New York: Grove Press, 1998), 270.

Chapter Eight

PASSOVER AND EXODUS AND THE METAPHORS WE LIVE BY

"If you really want to make a friend, go to someone's house and eat with him . . . the people who give you their food give you their heart."

—Cesar Chavez

Sometimes a single sentence in Scripture is packed with a lot of meaning. That's certainly the case with the line found in Exodus 1:8: "There arose a new king over Egypt, who did not know Joseph" (RSV). It comes early in Exodus, and it sets the tone for the theme of the book. In simple speak, this means that Joseph and his crowd went from being connected to being *persona non grata*. They went from free sideline tickets or backstage passes to the cheap seats. They went from the in-crowd to the out.

For a brief period in my life I worked in and around the United States Capitol Building in Washington. I served as a legislative fellow for a U.S. senator, and I learned that while pay on Capitol Hill is not great, the access is incredibly cool. For a year and half, along with the hard work and some long hours came the freedom to come and go largely as I pleased. I walked the gilded halls of the Brumidi Corridors, gave many behind-the-scenes tours to friends, took the underground subway between the Russell Senate Office Building and the capitol, and stood often in the U.S. Capitol Rotunda where our dead presidents have lain in state. Then one day my fellowship was over and with it my badge, parking sticker, keys, and access were gone. Poof. For a short while I still could accompany friends, but they were too busy for that, and the fact was that there was no need for me. Soon my former boss there, the chief of staff, had moved on to another job, so the powers that be *knew me not*. Soon I was driving by like any other tourist, locked out by well-armed government guards from the access that even the underlings with proximity to power enjoy.

That may be a lousy example but, if we magnified it a few hundred times, we might get close to understanding what happened to Joseph's family and relatives in Egypt once their guy Joseph and his friends had departed from office. The Bible has a word for departure: *Exodus*.

Just as Abraham was an improbable choice to lead the escape from Ur and the God/food issues there, so was Moses an unlikely candidate to take on the man-god Pharaoh. He had managed to kill a guy and go on the run and meet up with God in a bush in the wilderness. He rather reluctantly agreed to head back and have a talk with Pharaoh about renegotiating the age-old bad deal where the Jews set into motion a sequence of events that ended up trading future freedom for temporary food. The talks with Pharaoh go about like one might expect. They look a lot like a modern-day Monopoly game where the guy who owns only Baltic and Mediterranean has landed on a fat cat's Boardwalk property loaded with hotels. Except in this case, Moses the bankrupt player says to the Monopoly champ, "I'll give you one more chance. Here are the terms." As expected, Pharaoh bellows in reply, "You don't make the terms around here! I do."

That's when we see the God who loves to feed us at his best. He begins to systematically deal with the monopolizer, the hoarder, the tiny god-man Pharaoh by dismantling any false notion that Pharaoh can feed himself or his people. The Nile that Pharaoh managed with technological brilliance to bring crop abundance turns to blood. The sun that warmed the earth and coaxed seedlings from the loamy, Nile-soaked soil is blotted out, leaving the darkness in which nothing can grow. The cattle that brought meat and milk and cheese die, swarms of locusts gobble the crops, and hailstones ravage the lush fields. All this is but a warm-up for the final blow—God's ultimate plan to strip away the Egyptian means of production, their slaves. But in order for God to finally set the people of Israel free, he first insists on a grand reminder-meal, as if to set up a permanent touchstone for ages to come. Their stunted, enslaved, malnourished lives were about to be made right by the God who loves to feed them.

The first Passover meal involved the killing of lambs, their blood placed on Israeli doorposts, and bread prepared so hastily that it didn't even have time to rise. This meal ordained and prepared by God would serve as a touchstone for God's people for centuries thereafter. Indeed, it would be at the celebration of this annual meal many centuries later in Jerusalem that the God who loves to feed us would break into history with the culmination of his final plan to nourish his sons and daughters with a Bread of Life so powerful that they might never hunger again.

An entire book could be written on the power of food in the Passover, and indeed, many have been. For our purposes it is enough to note the fifty-thousand-foot level of perspective that the Passover provides us on God's work and wisdom, which is exactly what we might expect from a God who loves to feed us. It is a literal meal that becomes a centerpiece of the Jewish faith going forward. In contrast to the gods of the Egyptians who needed to be "fed" and offered up to on a quid pro quo arrangement, the God of Israel sits his people down for a meal. For generations to come, even to this day, the children ask at the Seder meal, "Grandfather, why is this night different than any other?" And the answer that comes resounding through the centuries, through the millennia, is the story of this meal. It was more than a mere tale to tell and retell. It is a story they can touch, a story they can taste, a story they can smell, a story that can both literally and metaphorically give life.

In 1980 George Lakoff wrote a now-classic book called *Metaphors We Live By.* In it, he argues convincingly that metaphor is essential to our thought processes, present in every conversation, the core to the way we make sense of the world we live in. While Lakoff is not concerned with Scripture, Scripture is certainly concerned with metaphor. In fact, it is absolutely full of metaphor. But it's important to note that as we attempt to understand the many metaphors in the Bible, this metaphor, the metaphor of hunger, nourishment, and feeding, goes beyond metaphor and is transcendental. Let me tell you what I mean:

To begin with, take a second to look up the word *parable* in a dictionary and the definition will tell you that parables are *extended metaphors.* Jesus knew Lakoff was right before Lakoff knew it. Jesus did not preach or teach like we teach, or like the teachers of his day, for that matter. He offered his listeners extended metaphors, knowing they would connect with them and discover the deeper meaning behind them. The parables he told extemporaneously stand today as some of the most profound in history.

Jesus may have been the best in his use of these extended metaphors to inspire and teach people, but he was not the first. The Old Testament is full of rich and powerful metaphors as well. Jesus and his followers took up that mantle and crafted more word pictures of their own. The Bible, from beginning to end, is teeming with these powerful metaphors.

With all of these metaphors running amok in Scripture, modern eyes now view these holy writings though many lenses. Perhaps first and foremost in the West, Scripture now is seen as fairy tale. It is interesting, perhaps for historical purposes, we are told, but only taken as "true" by people who long to find in these pages some meaning or who wish to validate a faith given them by parents or culture. And since these faith-people are determined to find some cryptic meaning in the texts, they do. Those who think the Bible is mostly fairy tale don't see it as a book of salvation. In fact, just the opposite. In the hands of zealots, the Bible is viewed (and books perceive to be like it, such as the Koran) as the source of most of the conflict in the world today. Every bit of it was meant to be metaphorical, they might say. And foolish people have gone and taken these strange words literally. Therein lies the problem, some modern folks firmly believe.

Others have a slightly kinder, gentler view of the Bible. They see Scripture as a useful historical narrative but, like all old documents, written from a skewed perspective. It's worthy of study because of the undeniable impact it has had on the world, but calling it divine or inspired is not helpful if one seeks to find in these old writings some headway in making sense of history. To this crowd, Lakoff's book title is especially apropos. "These are metaphors we live by." For sure. But these metaphors are not alive, nor do they contain life, these folks insist. Not in a real sense anyway. That would be silly, and impossible. Metaphors are powerful and inspirational, but not that powerful. They are just useful rhetorical tools.

The remaining group consists of those of us who think the Bible is God's word to a world that desperately needs some good news and some direction. Granted, within this group one finds a wide range of readers—all the way from those who strive to take each word literally to those who think only *some* of the words of Jesus are actually inspired. This wide-ranging camp is my camp, and I grew up far closer to the literalist side than to the other. I was born here among "the born again," and I can't shake both the feeling and the conviction that the Bible is something special, something true, something inspired, something more than a mere book of nice *metaphors we live by.*

It is my assumption that the majority of those reading this far into this book are somewhere in the latter camp along with me. That is, you actually think the Bible is God's word and seek to find there not only good advice for everyday life but also eternal truths from the sovereign God of the universe. If you are in the other camp, I'm impressed that you made it this far without getting a bit bored with my repetitive premise. But for the Bible-believing crowd, or for those who have some small spark in their heart that wonders if the Bible really is inspired, this premise of a God who loves to feed us is intended to offer a new lens through which to read the Bible and attempt to make sense of it. In this book I am arguing that the Scriptures contain a clear, persistent, coherent theme that most of us have missed. Once we do identify it, we are then surprised—even stunned—to see how pervasive it is. It just keeps popping up at every turn, in every story, in nearly every book and chapter. This ubiquitous theme is simply this: that we serve a God who loves to feed us, and our nourishment is one of his chief concerns.

It's important to add here that there are indeed many themes or metaphors in Scripture that can be seen from beginning to end. One is that of salvation, the concept that we are lost or broken creatures who need to be rescued or saved. Another is similar, but a bit different—that we humans are alienated from heaven, in need of reconciliation but unable to broker the deal on our own. These are just two, but there are others. It is not my intent to attempt to supersede any of them or to argue that this particular lens for reading Scripture is superior to others or should become the new primary lens. Obviously I am convinced that thinking of God and the Bible as nourishing humanity is helpful, but if it doesn't help you, then drop it. I am not astute enough or profound enough to offer anything truly new here in this book. If I claimed to do so, it would likely be a good clue for you to quit reading right now.

Having said that, I do think that the theme of a God who loves to feed us is more than just a nice sermon series. In *Metaphors We Live By,* Lakoff points out that it's hard for us to talk about anything meaningful without quickly resorting to metaphor. It's just how the human brain works. We know from our junior high school English classes that a simile is a type of metaphor, a rhetorical device that uses "like" or "as" to make a point. Both within and outside of his longer parables, Jesus used this rhetorical device all the time. He would say, "It's like a farmer who sowed seeds by a path," or, "like a mustard seed." But he also dispensed with simile and spoke more directly at times. "You *are* the light of the world," he said to his disciples. He didn't say, "You are like light." He said, "You *are* light." Moreover, in talking about himself, he never said, "I am like bread." Instead, he said, "I *am* the Bread of Life." These were not metaphors in the normal sense, in the way our English teachers (bless their hearts!) sought for us to understand them. In the case of our being "light," we are left to contemplate the implications. We know we don't mystically become actual light waves in a literal sense. So in that regard it was, and is, metaphor. But we also know it is more than that. And when he speaks of himself and his work and who he actually was (and is), these statements go beyond metaphor. We really don't fully understand it, because we don't have any experience in any other facet of our lives where this sort of supernatural happening takes place.

My point here is that Jesus and his followers who wrote about him in what became the Bible used all sorts of metaphors. And when we consider these metaphors today, in modern times, quite a few of them have started to lose their punch. *I was lost, but now I am found. I was blind, but now I see. I was in prison. I was a slave.* I rarely meet anyone today who has had these experiences in a literal sense. My wife called me not long ago and said, "I am lost." My first reaction was to say, "Where are you?" She had made a wrong turn and was unable to look at Google Maps on her phone as she drove, so she called. She was not really lost in the sense that people of old got lost. In the old days being lost meant you could get eaten by an animal or you could starve or freeze to death in the elements. Today it just means you made a wrong turn and will be a little late, or your battery died in an unfamiliar part of town. So the concept of true "lostness" is, forgive the pun, lost on us. Similarly, I don't personally know anyone who is blind, and I know very, very few who once were prisoners. (Sad commentary on me, I know. Jesus knew lots of them and died as one.) I am suggesting that all of these metaphors have lost some of their punch for modern America because we have to think of them mostly in a metaphorical sense. I was a prisoner to that particular habit; I was lost in the way I pursued the wrong proverbial path. All these figures of speech are true and even quite profound to us at times, but it's hard for them to resonate at our core as they did for people of old, because most of us have not personally experienced those sorts of hardships. I can't shake the feeling that when you have to think of a metaphor in a metaphorical sense, some part of the capacity to grasp it is diminished. We don't have intense, deeply personal memories and bouts with many of the metaphors of Scripture, so we run the risk of failing to be as deeply impacted by them as people of old may have been.

But the Passover is different. It's deeper, more powerful than just a story, because there is one metaphor in Scripture that we do encounter in a deeply personal way every single day, usually three times a day. That is the daily reality of hunger. Hunger is there waiting for us each day when we wake up, and it prods many of us into ill-advised late-night snacks before we go to bed. It haunts rich and poor, geniuses and fools, healthy and sick. I think God knew this when he freed the slaves in Egypt and instituted this meal as a way to mark the occasion. I think Jesus knew it was much more than a metaphor when he said, "I am the Bread of Life." The disciples who first heard this were deeply confused and disturbed. "How can we eat your flesh and drink your blood?" they wondered. "This is a hard teaching," they said. So hard, in fact, that when he said it, most of the crowd who heard it left him. He could have calmed them by saying, "Guys, guys, calm down. It was just a metaphor!" But he didn't. He watched the crowd leave, and then he looked at his disciples and said, "What about you? Are you leaving as well?"

By this time you must be completely sick of the word *metaphor*, so I will end here. This phenomenon that I am perhaps doing a rather poor job explaining has long haunted Christian theologians in regard to the Eucharist. Debates about transubstantiation and consubstantiation were heated and passionate and divisive in Luther's time. *How did this "I am the Bread of Life" thing really work when we took the Lord's Supper?* they wondered. Some said he literally was present in the bread and the wine. Others said it was symbolic. One thing is for sure, we remain a bit confused about it to this day. I think the God who loves to feed us looks at the confusion and says, "Good! They are pondering literal versus spiritual food. Got them right where I want them!"

Chapter Nine

WILDERNESS FOOD

"Truly we met God in each other and while sharing food."

—Arthur Paul Boers

After centuries of slavery, the people of Israel were now free. They learned that unfortunately this newfound freedom had its downsides as well. The biggest and most pressing downside was hunger. While slavery under the Egyptians was no walk in the park, at least the food was plentiful. Just as farmers today pour fuel in their tractors, the Egyptians kept their slaves fed and strong. Yet this harsh new desert was a far cry from the rich fertile soil of the Nile River basin.

Before long, Moses' band of emigrants began to do what many of us do when God does not provide circumstances that suit us. They griped. In the desert the whole community grumbled against Moses and Aaron. The Israelites said to their leaders, "If only we had died by the LORD's hand in Egypt! There we sat around pots of meat and ate all the food we wanted, but you have brought us out into this desert to starve this entire assembly to death" (Exod. 16:2–3).

After centuries of slavery, it took them all of about a month of camping in the desert to start complaining. Apparently in this case the griping worked, because God replied not just favorably, but lavishly. In fact, we are left to wonder whether God allowed them to get into a tough spot so they would ask exactly the question he wanted so he could unfold his plan. "God, we are hungry!" they cried. "Okay," God said. "Food is on the way!"

> Then the LORD said to Moses, "I will rain down bread from heaven for you. The people are to go out each day and gather enough for that day. In this way I will test them and see whether they will follow my instructions. On the sixth day they are to prepare what they bring in, and that is to be twice as much as they gather on the other days."
>
> So Moses and Aaron said to all the Israelites, "In the evening you will know that it was the LORD who brought you out of Egypt, and in the morning you will see the glory of the LORD, because he has heard your grumbling against him. Who are

> we, that you should grumble against us?" Moses also said, "You will know that it was the LORD when he gives you meat to eat in the evening and all the bread you want in the morning, because he has heard your grumbling against him. Who are we? You are not grumbling against us, but against the LORD."
>
> Then Moses told Aaron, "Say to the entire Israelite community, 'Come before the LORD, for he has heard your grumbling.'" While Aaron was speaking to the whole Israelite community, they looked toward the desert, and there was the glory of the LORD appearing in the cloud. The LORD said to Moses, "I have heard the grumbling of the Israelites. Tell them, 'At twilight you will eat meat, and in the morning you will be filled with bread. Then you will know that I am the LORD your God.'" That evening quail came and covered the camp, and in the morning there was a layer of dew around the camp. When the dew was gone, thin flakes like frost on the ground appeared on the desert floor. When the Israelites saw it, they said to each other, "What is it?" For they did not know what it was. (Exod. 16:4–15)

They did not have a word for this new flaky stuff on the ground, so they called it "manna," or "whatchamacallit." It's a hilarious picture really. They walked out of their tents hungry, found something on the ground, and asked, "Hey, what is this stuff?"

One of the more brave (or hungry) ones decided to try eating it, and they loved it. Soon they were sitting around munching on it, saying, "Hey, pass me a little more of that 'what-is-it-manna' stuff."

It's hard to miss the fact that God has anti-monopoly legislation attached to this unlimited bread deal. The God who loves to feed them is saying to them, "Don't be like Pharaoh with my bread. Don't hoard it. There is plenty to go around. Just gather enough for the day and trust me that I will show up again tomorrow and rain more free food on your grumbling heads." Sure enough, they fail the test, and when they do, the hoarded bread turns rotten. He tells them to rest on the Sabbath, and so they need to collect double on the day before. Some ignore this commandment too, only to show up hungry on the Sabbath and find nothing.

Moses tells them to gather a bit of the "what is it?" and put it in a Ziploc and some tinfoil, and this sample ends up in the Ark of the Covenant alongside the stone tablets that contain the Ten Commandments. God is determined that future grumblers remember this story and have it as a continual reminder that when they pray prayers like "give us this day our daily bread," God is listening. Only three things are worthy of being placed within the ultra-holy Ark. The ten rules of the Lord, reminding them that he has expectations. The budding rod of Aaron, to remind them that not just any Tom, Dick, or Harry can be a legitimate priest. And the jar of manna, to make it clear that they serve a God who loves to feed them.

This manna/quail feeding goes on for forty years. Manna, the "bread of heaven," falls night after night, and they rise every weekday morning to scoop it up and eat it. It's hard for me to imagine eating the same thing over and over again for that long. As I mentioned earlier, I run an organization called MANA Nutrition, an organization that makes little packets of peanut butter for severely malnourished children in developing countries. At one point, early on in our process of launching MANA, I decided I would eat nothing but MANA for a month. After all, that's what we ask mothers to do with their children, to feed them a six-week regimen of MANA, feeding them three packets a day. If I believed in our product, I figured the least I could do was to eat it by prescription as I expected our end user to eat it.

I started down this path and made it about three days before I was completely sick of the thought of extracting peanut butter from a package into my mouth for yet another meal, so I backtracked on my commitment and altered it a bit. I would still eat MANA, but I would allow myself one time a day when I could put it on bread or on a banana. I stayed on this MANA fast for about twenty-five days. Along the way I dropped fifteen pounds, a far cry from the huge weight gains we were seeing for the kids in Africa, who could nearly double their weight in a month by eating our MANA concoction.

If I was sick of my MANA after less than forty days, I can imagine how sick the Israelites must have been of eating the same old manna. While the Bible never says that's *all* they had to eat for forty years, it does say that they are rather quick to start complaining about it. By the very next chapter, Exodus

17, they are complaining—not about the food, though, but about water, a concern which might very well have been legit, since humans don't last long without water. God fixed this for them when Moses whacked a rock with a stick and water flowed out. By chapter 20, Moses headed up onto Mt. Sinai to get the Ten Commandments. He stayed up there for a while, forty days to be exact. Which amounts to twelve chapters of Bible for us. And Exodus 32:1 tells us, "When the people saw that Moses was so long in coming down from the mountain, they gathered around Aaron and said, 'Come, make us gods who will go before us. As for this fellow Moses who brought us up out of Egypt, we don't know what has happened to him.'"

"This fellow Moses" had disappeared on them. They were sick of waiting around and wanted a God who would feed them. So what did they do? They fashioned a God who could feed them, a golden-calf god. It's hard to miss the symbolism here. In fact, it appears that the Israelites are not quite clever enough at this point to be symbolic at all. They are literal in their interpretation of the ideal god. A god they could milk. A god who would give them cheese, and meat to eat, and butter for some real bread instead of manna, and yogurt and cream for dessert—a complete dairy-god.

Moses came down the mountain and was apoplectic when he saw how quickly they had sold out to their bellies. He found them dancing after they had "sat down to eat and drink and indulge in revelry," so he smashed his new stone tablets in anger and, in verse 20, melted down the new calf-god they had fashioned and made them eat it. Actually he pounded the idol into powder and made them drink it. But whatever the case, it was a hilarious (and sad) ending to their god who would feed them. Moses turned the tables on them and fed their fake god to them. I can just imagine them choking down this gold-ash-smoothie he made for them, and then I can see them struggling to keep it down. It's not in Scripture, but Moses must have been saying, "There you go! How's that taste? Is that what you wanted from your god?"

What is truly sad here is that the people of Israel had jumped the gun and had not realized what was happening up on the mountain. While "this fellow Moses" was away up on the mountain, he was in an intense planning session with the God who loved to feed them. In Exodus 23, God gave Moses a directive for three feasts. Three generous, mandated holiday parties and feasts much better and more lavish than the one they had fashioned for themselves with the man-made calf-god. The three festivals are *Pesach* (Passover), *Shavuot,* and *Sukkot.* In the Hebrew they are referred to as *Shalosh HaRegalim.*

The first was the Feast of Unleavened Bread. It is now called Pesach, a feast they already had from Exodus 12. It marked two things: the early harvesting of the barley and the release of the children of Israel from bondage. It came in the spring, celebrated a spring harvest time, and lasted for seven days.

While the first feast marked the first grain harvest, the second one noted in Exodus 23:16 is the Festival of the Harvest. It would come to be called *Shavuot.* It marked the last spring grain harvest and the first fruit harvest, seven weeks after the second day of Pesach. For this reason it would also be called the feast of "first fruits." This feast would also mark the day that the Torah would be given to the Jewish people.

A major feature of the future celebrations of this feast would be the ceremony of bringing the "first fruits," or *bikkurim*, of the harvest to the temple as an offering of thanks to God. Note that they would come *to thank God for feeding them*—not to feed God so he would spare them. They were to look back with thankfulness, not look forward with fear and anxiety. These *bikkurim* would be carried in beautifully decorated baskets, as families gathered together and walked to Jerusalem, singing and dancing and playing music as they walked. When they arrived at the temple, they would hand over the bread and fruit to the priests, who would bless these offerings. Today synagogues are decorated with greenery and flowers on *Shavuot.* Tradition has it that King David was born and died on *Shavuot.* In fact, today many students in Jewish schools have their graduation on *Shavuot.*

The third feast was also about food and harvests. It was called the "Festival of Tabernacles" or *Sukkot.* It is also referred to as *Chag haAsif*, or the Festival of Gathering. This feast as well became associated with the major event in their history, the Exodus from Egypt when the Israelites lived in tent-like temporary dwellings. It is a fall festival of gathering. This feast takes place when all the fruits of the orchards have been gathered as winter approaches. It is sometimes referred to as *Z'man Simchatenu* (The Time of Our Happiness). Moses instructed the children of Israel to gather for a reading of the Law during *Sukkot* every seventh year (Deut. 31:10–11). King Solomon dedicated the temple in Jerusalem on *Sukkot*

(1 Kings 8; 2 Chron. 7). And *Sukkot* was the first sacred occasion observed after the resumption of sacrifices in Jerusalem following the Babylonian captivity (Ezra 3:4).

Later, after the temple was built in Jerusalem, these three feasts became "Pilgrim Feasts." The Jews would make pilgrimages from far and wide to come pray at the temple. The whole system would prove to be much better, more lavish, and more celebratory than they ever could have imagined as they sat and ate their small meal around their man-made golden calf-god. They imagined the best party possible and threw it for themselves, right when the God who loved to feed them was planning to do something infinitely better.

All of this was in the plans for them as early as Exodus 23, but in chapter 32 we find them literally eating and drinking the awful crushed-up ashes of their calf-god. They were like kids having their mouths washed out with soap, only worse. Moses, having just come from a conference with the holy God, was incensed, and it was as if he said to them, "You think your homemade, make-believe gods can feed you? I'll feed that god to you instead!"

Chapter Ten

JUBILEE

"Hunger is not a problem. It is an obscenity. How wonderful it is that nobody need wait a single moment before starting to improve the world."

—Anne Frank

The fashioning of their own cow-god is nearly the last straw for the God who loves to feed them. In the following chapter he tells them, "Since I promised long ago, go ahead and go to the land flowing with milk and honey, but I am not going with you. In fact, I just might destroy you on the way." Moses meets with God and says, "If you are not going, don't send us." God sends Moses back up the mountain, and this time he comes back down with his face glowing. Exodus then ends with a rather detailed account of what the newly assembled tabernacle ends up looking like.

When we move on to Leviticus, the first twenty-four chapters probably are the best argument against my "God who loves to feed us" refrain, because they seem to detail not only a long list of stuff the Jews are forbidden to eat (chapter 11), but they also impose an almost unending list of laws and specifications on how to offer various sacrifices to God. Grain offerings, animal offerings, internal organs, blood, instructions on how to present bread and olive oil to God. You name it and there seems to be one particular way to do it, and serious ramifications for you if you get it wrong. Leviticus 10 tells of the tragic time when Aaron's sons Nadab and Abihu get turned into toast because of their "strange offerings."

Since we have the benefit of having the end of the story to read as well, we can see later that the people of Israel remain consistent in their tendency to miss the point. They certainly do miss the point of all these offerings. "Do you think I need this stuff?" God will ask them later in Isaiah 1:11. "'The multitude of your sacrifices—what are they to me?' says the LORD. 'I have more than enough of burnt offerings, of rams and the fat of fattened animals; I have no pleasure in the blood of bulls and lambs and goats.'"

Indeed, while the Jews wholeheartedly buy into the rules and regulations given in the first twenty chapters of Leviticus, historians tell us that they likely never get around to actually putting Leviticus 25 into practice. This extraordinary chapter institutes an amazing concept and command by God that was to be followed every fifty years. It was called the Year of

Jubilee. The Year of Jubilee, or "the year of the Lord's favor" was to be a giant "reset" button for the entire community. All Israelite slaves were to go free, all debts were to be forgiven, all land went back to its original owner. (It is interesting to note, isn't it, that our Liberty Bell in Philadelphia has a portion of Leviticus 25:10 forged upon it: "Proclaim liberty throughout all the land unto all the inhabitants thereof.")

Biblical historian Roland de Vaux writes concerning the Year of Jubilee:

> There is no evidence that the law was ever in fact applied. . . . The Law of Jubilee thus appears to set out an ideal of justice and social equality which was never realized. It is difficult to say when it was thought out. . . . But we must note that nowhere outside the Bible is the fiftieth year marked by a redistribution of the land or a remission of debts and of persons taken as sureties; nor is there any evidence whatever of such a general liberation, at any time whatever.[1]

So it appears that the people of Israel never quite had the guts to pull this one off. Indeed, in spite of our etching it on the Liberty Bell, I have a hard time imagining a command that would be less popular to modern Americans. All prisoners free! All debts forgiven!

But imagine a community that did put it into practice. At least in the early years after Jubilee, there would be no marginalized population, no hunger, no disparity between the haves and have-nots. A fifty-year clock would tick and, as it did, at least once in most lifetimes it would reset and revamp everything in their economic status. In such a world the pharaonic monopoly mentality would be dead in its tracks. In such a world hoarding makes little sense. Jubilee is as good as manna from heaven really. The God who loves to feed us is stepping in and rendering all things fair and all people fed.

The implications for a society that reset everything every fifty years are hard to fully comprehend. Debts forgiven, prisoners free (according to the Greek translation Jesus read that day in Nazareth; the original Hebrew spoke of freedom for the "oppressed"). It's radical stuff, and it certainly tests my American sensibilities and fundamental beliefs about personal wealth and ownership. Jubilee has many implications, but perhaps the most radical aspect is the idea that land would be returned. Now everyone would be more focused on using their plots, not necessarily to sell and generate short-term cash, but to build up a sustainable mechanism to feed and improve their families and communities. And, if someone did sell off a property, it would only be a fifty-year lease. If improvements were made to that land, the builder would reap the benefits and the seller would live off the sale price (if he negotiated wisely). Then the original owner would pass by the property with his grandchildren and say to them, "Wow! Look what our friend is building for you!"

In recent years economist Hernando de Soto won a Nobel Prize for noting that a lack of property rights for peasant farmers is perhaps the biggest limiting factor for the poorest on our globe. De Soto noted that many of the peasants actually own property, but they have no deeds, no legal proof of ownership, that might allow them to use their land as collateral and get some value out of it. De Soto noted that if governments ascribed value and official legal ownership to land, then poor peasant farmers would immediately have access to huge amounts of previously untapped capital reserves to improve, build on, and add value to their lives. It could not be taken away, squatted on, or drained of its minerals, and the poor could then join the world economy and tap this value the way we do in more developed countries where property rights are strong.

While the Year of Jubilee was never enacted by the Jews, as far as we know, it would finally be declared by a bold Jewish rabbi in Luke 4. In what might be the first sermon Jesus ever preached, in his hometown synagogue, Jesus opened the Scripture and declared "the year of our Lord's favor." The prisoner set free. All things made new. This declaration set off a chain of events that changed the world like none before. It launched a ministry that would make it continually and abundantly clear that we serve a God who loves to feed us.

Note

[1]Roland de Vaux, *Ancient Israel*, 2 vols. (New York: McGraw-Hill, 1965), vol. 1, 175.

Chapter Eleven

NOT BY BREAD ALONE

"There is no sincerer love than the love of food."

—George Bernard Shaw

"Man cannot live by bread alone, but by every word that proceeds from the mouth of YHWH." That's how Moses summarized the lessons learned by the Israelites while they wandered for forty years in the wilderness (Deut. 8:3). It is interesting that Jesus quotes this statement in the New Testament during his own wilderness experience. Both times these words are meant to show the importance of God as the life-giver, but the use of the word "alone" also acknowledges that bread is necessary for life. We humans can't last much more than a month without bread and less than a week without water.

The older testament is the original home to many of the metaphors we later see in the newer one, and this is especially true of food and hunger metaphors. Our Christian Bible contains the Old and the New Testaments, and the English words "old" and "new" used in their titles are loaded with meaning for Americans who value the "newest, latest, greatest" so highly. When something is *old* in America, it is often considered useless. "That's my old cell phone. My old VCR." Thereby we designate relics that have been technologically bypassed by the newer, better, truer, more useful versions. This "too-good-to-throw-away" reality provides inventory for endless garage sales and clutters storage units across the land. That's why it's helpful for us to remember that what we call the "Old" Testament actually might better be called the "older" testament. If I introduce my brother Mike as my "old brother," it's either an insult, a quip, or a sign that he has somehow ceased to be my brother. But if I say he is my "older" brother, then the word choice communicates respect and an honored place for him in my life and family.

In the Older Testament, as we have noticed in the early chapters of this book, there seems to be a dominant and recurring theme of food, nourishment, and provision. For our purposes of supporting the "God who loves to feed us" theme, we are only three books into the Scriptures, and we have already had to skip dozens of food stories and verses that could provide extra chapters in this book. For the sake of time, we won't hunt through the rest of the Older Testament mentioning each one, but some major highlights do deserve a mention.

The provision of a land flowing with milk and honey is the promise God makes and keeps to his people. We have considered this metaphor. Before and after he makes good on this promise, however, few pages in the Older Testament fail to mention food. Indeed, food provides some of the most important social, political, and religious symbols in the Bible. Many of these symbols are familiar to us—symbols like the forbidden fruit in the Garden of Eden and the land flowing with milk and honey. But the breadth of biblical symbolism associated with food reaches beyond these famous examples. We see food and nurture popping up all over when we examine the text. Whether it is the distinct link between food and memory in Deuteronomy, the confusion of food and warfare in Judges, the great importance of feasting in the Israelite monarchy, the literary motif of divine judgment at the table, the use of food in the formation of Israelite identity in the post-exilic period, or just the overall healthiness of the ancient Israelite diet, the food and hunger themes abound.

But just in case we are not quite sharp enough to tease out themes as our English teachers hoped we would, the Bible includes some plain old in-your-face hunger stories that even we simpletons can't miss. In addition to Cain and Abel fighting (and killing) over food/God issues, and the later brothers Jacob and Esau fighting over soup, there are so many more. Ruth gleans for food, Elijah is fed by ravens, David and his men eat the holy bread reserved for the priests.

The Jewish psalms are equally plainspoken with repeated references to God feeding his people. The most famous psalm, the twenty-third, includes praise of the great Shepherd who leaves no wants. "You prepare a table before me," David sings. Then there is the preceding psalm, Psalm 22, an uncanny prophecy written in 1000 BC that Christ quoted on the cross, beginning with, "My God, my God, why have you forsaken me?" and ending with, "It is finished!" As it foretells things to be ushered in by God's ultimate Deliverer, verse 26 predicts, "The poor will eat and be satisfied." Later there is Psalm 136:3, 25, "Give thanks to the Lord of lords . . . who gives food to every creature. His love endures forever." Again in Psalm 146:7 we read of the Lord, "He gives justice to the poor . . . and feeds the hungry" (TLB). Dozens more reflect on hunger and on the Lord's ability to feed us.

Isaiah implores God's people that they should "pour [themselves] out for the hungry" (58:10). Isaiah 58 might best be titled, "The Fast I Choose." The themes of food and hunger pervade the chapter. Fasting was evidently a common practice at the time, but only among those with enough food. The poor fast by necessity, not by choice. The fast God "chooses" is, ironically, to provide food for the hungry. In doing so, he enables them to break their enforced fast.

We have mentioned but a fraction of the Older Testament's references and themes that engage issues of food, hunger, and provision, but hopefully the point is made. They served, as we serve today, a God who loved to feed people. As the Older Testament closes and gives way to a new story, it closes with one of the most powerful stories of food and faith. God's people are back in the land of the Chaldeans, back near Ur in the land between the rivers, not far from where it all started and where food production first exploded. The new champion of faith is Daniel, and he will face and stand firm against a king who tries to force-feed him his food and another who tries to turn him into food for his lions.

Chapter Twelve

AMONG THE LIONS

"It's difficult to think anything but pleasant thoughts while eating a homegrown tomato."

—Lewis Grizzard

The opening verses of the book of Daniel lay out the plot. King Nebuchadnezzar brings in some sharp young guys from his latest group of captives, and one of them happens to be a young man named Daniel. The king's goal is to immerse Daniel and his companions in three years of training in Babylonian language and culture. In order to provide a healthy environment, verse 5 explains, "The king assigned them a daily amount of wine and food from the king's table."

Then three verses later the historian tells us that Daniel refused "to defile himself with the royal food and wine."

The food here and Daniel's restraint due to his faith are centerpieces of this story. Daniel would become one of the great heroes of the Jewish faith.

At the time when I am writing this book, a phenomenon called the "Daniel diet" is popular among U.S. evangelicals. Championed by Saddleback Church, it offers what seems like fairly right-headed advice on eating an alternative diet to the typical American high-sugar, high-carb, high-calorie diet. "Eat like Daniel," it says. "Resist the bad food temptations of the culture, and you'll live a happier, healthier life."

While I have no problem with the Daniel diet in name or in concept, the historical context of the book of Daniel seems to suggest that the diet he chose in Babylon had little to do with health. Daniel scholar and Professor of Old Testament at Princeton Theological Seminary Choon-Leong Seow agrees, and reminds us that Daniel is not so much a story of resisting rich food as it is a story of resisting a rich foreign king. Daniel and his friends resist the king's food, Seow says, as a tangible expression of their reliance on God's power instead of the king's. Daniel and his friends need to establish their own identity. They accept the silly names the Chaldeans gave them, but the one thing they could reject was the privilege of the king's food.

One school of thought would say that the Babylonian diet had some exotic tastes uncommon (and indeed forbidden) to Jewish tables: horse, cat, camel, and dog are Babylonian meats forbidden in Leviticus. Add the obvious pork to the list and the likelihood that the creature had not been slaughtered properly and Daniel and his friends could well have been looking at a short list of kosher options. Better to be safe than sorry, and besides, who knew if the king's food had been offered to idols—another thing that would have made it off-limits to the young Jews.

The above list of rather odd tastes notwithstanding, a much longer list of meats would have been just fine. Wine would have also been okay. What if, for Daniel, a diet of legumes was a way to remain faithful in the face of the overwhelming power of the Babylonians, a culture that, as we have noted earlier, was still famous for its prowess and ability to generate food. Seow says it well: "The point is not the triumph of vegetarianism or even the triumph of piety or the triumph of wisdom, but the triumph of God."[1]

It's easy here to look back and see the similarities of this story and the story of Joseph. Both were Jewish boys captured and sent to serve foreign kings. Both were tempted with the riches of a king's court—Daniel with decadent food and wine, Joseph with the beauty of an official's wife. In both cases they rejected the privileges they were offered and refused to compromise God's role in their lives. In both cases a clear message was sent to their adopted community that they served a different sort of God than the Babylonians and Egyptians were used to. In Daniel's case it was a literal rejection of the food of the culture in favor of the food of a God who loved to feed him.

Whether or not we want to use the Daniel story to preach about healthy living, the eat-vegetables-and-whole-foods [illegible]ation is neither an egregious violation of the text nor a bad idea. Certainly the willpower and commitment Daniel showed is a great example, as we live in a culture with plenty of temptations and unhealthy attitudes about food.

Perhaps more than anything else we derive from the Daniel story, the call for restraint and for consciously choosing not to get drunk on excess is the book's most powerful message. This attitude and approach to our food would benefit, not only the privileged, but also the needy, who tend to get society's leftovers. Resisting a rich king is not easy, and the king's rich food is likely one of the simpler, more direct temptations of that king. More important than that is having enough faith and good sense to resist the urge to think like that foreign king.

Believing that we can be filled, nourished, and sustained with anything or anyone other than the God who loves to feed us is the primary lie of our culture today. Pursuit of knowing more, feeling better, looking better, or buying more won't fill us up or give us energy to sustain and fuel the life-gift within us. That is the work of the God who loves to feed us.

Note

[1]Choon-Leong Seow, *Daniel* (Louisville, KY: Westminster John Knox Press, 2003), 28.

Chapter Thirteen

IF I WERE HUNGRY, I WOULD NOT TELL YOU

"It is better to sleep with an empty stomach than with a troubled heart."

—Ugandan proverb

One thing I learned from living in East Africa for nearly a decade was that my dependence on sarcasm to get a laugh is a hit-or-miss proposition (mostly a miss, unfortunately). Stemming from an overreliance on sarcastic humor, my idea of what was funny fell flat over and over again.

It's impressive, then, to see sarcasm translate as clearly and effectively as it does in some biblical writings. In Psalm 50, for example, leaping through time and nimbly navigating culture and linguistic barriers are words dripping with sarcasm and wit. After using dramatic terms in an attempt to put the Almighty's true expectations in perspective, in Psalm 50:12 God asks rhetorically (my paraphrase), "If I were hungry and needed something to eat, would I tell you?" This is especially interesting language (and clever, I think) in an ancient world where people seemed obsessed with feeding their gods. It follows similar language found in Deuteronomy 32:37–38, where the author makes fun of other gods by asking, "Where are their gods . . . who ate the fat of your sacrifices? . . . Let them rise up and help you!" (TEV).

Psalm 50 reads like a perfect proof text to support the view of a God who seeks not to be fed, but to feed. In Psalm 50, as a response to those who placed all their religious marbles on the observance of the ceremonial law and thought such a bet sufficient, the psalmist pulled out the original contract between God and Israel, in which both parties were assigned their respective roles: "Hear, O my people! and I will speak" (50:7). The problem seemed to be that while they were ready to hear any good news he might have for them, they were less than eager to listen up when he testified against them and called them on the carpet for missing the point.

In Psalm 50:8–13, the psalmist makes clear God's view of their legalistic attitude toward sacrifices. Their problem was not neglect of these ceremonial institutions; in fact, it was just the opposite: they had been more than dutiful in their observance of them. Their burnt offerings were faithfully placed before God with great pride and ceremony. The problem was that they seemed to think these constant sacrifices would excuse their neglect of the weightier matters of the Law. In fact, what became clear was that if they had neglected the ceremonial sacrifices and failed to check the "sacrifice" box, it seemed to them that it might have been a smaller offense than their overdependence upon these rituals. It was as if they thought God was beholden to them for the many offerings they had brought to his altar. They had managed to make him their debtor by feeding him so well. With biting sarcasm the author of this psalm points out that it is not as if God could not have maintained his affairs without their contributions.

The Creator did not need their sacrifices. Why would he need their bulls and goats when he commanded all the beasts of the forest, and the cattle on a thousand hills (50:9–10)? Did he need them to show up with a small goat for his lunch when he had incontestable dominion over every beast on earth? As the psalmist reminds us, *"Every one of these depends on you to give them daily food. You supply it, and they gather it.* You open wide your hand to feed them, and they are satisfied with all your bountiful provision" (Ps. 104:27–28 TLB, emphasis mine).

In Psalm 50 we see that God's infinite self-sufficiency only served to prove their utter insufficiency and inability to add anything to him. He could not and did not benefit from their sacrifices and their goodness. It did not rub off on him in some way, nor was he any better off for it.

To counter this attitude, God made it clear that his infinite Spirit could not be supported by meat and drink, as human bodies can be. He did not need a snack or even three square meals. Instead, he reminded them, "to obey is better than sacrifice" (1 Sam. 15:22), and to love God and our neighbor better than all burnt offerings.

In an effort to drive this message home even further, he let them know that his favorite sacrifices were prayer and praise, and he called them preferable to all burnt offerings and sacrifices (Ps. 50:14–15). Furthermore, he reminded them that a healthy dose of self-awareness and honest confession of their sins would go a long way with him: A broken and contrite heart was the sacrifice God would not despise (Ps. 51:17). He reminded them that if their lives were not lived out with honest attempts to be right and just, then their sin offerings would not be acceptable. And finally, a few psalms later, he told them that just being grateful to him would impress him the most:

> I will praise God's name in song and glorify him with thanksgiving. This will please the LORD more than an ox, more than a bull with its horns and hooves. (Ps. 69:30–31)

Unfortunately, this repeated message does not sink in very deep, and they continue their adventures in missing the point. The Old Testament closes with prophets and locusts and more stories about food and the famines. Isaiah talks about it, as do Amos, Jeremiah, and Micah. God uses his prophets to remind them continually that their sacrifices not only are unacceptable, but they are sickening to him if they come from people who are living in sin. Instead of pleasing him, he saw their offerings as a mockery, as an affront to him. Hear this message over and over in passages like Proverbs 15:8; Isaiah

1:11–23; 66:3; Jeremiah 6:20; or Amos 5:21. God warns them repeatedly not to take much stock in these god-feeding performances, but instead to conduct themselves in everyday ways that show reverence toward him as their God. Finally, seemingly frustrated that his prophets are not being heeded, the Almighty strikes the final blow, and the God who loves to feed us becomes bread himself. In case they have missed the Nourish theme up to this point, he ensures that from this point onward they will not.

Chapter Fourteen

ARAUNAH'S FLOOR

"To be interested in food but not in food production is clearly absurd."

—**Wendell Berry**

Most of us who are moderately familiar with the Bible know the story of Elijah being fed by ravens. If you are like me, you tend to forget exactly where it's at or why it's there, or if it was actually Elijah or Elisha . . . but it's a famous story. It's one of those random Bible stories that is just offbeat and odd enough to stick somewhere in our memories.

What is really cool for our purposes here is to look at the story in its context and in the context of our wider conversation about how much God loves to feed his people. You can find this story in 1 Kings 17, but a context of sorts begins in the closing paragraphs of the previous book in the Bible, 2 Samuel. There King David builds an altar to the Lord, and to do so he is instructed to buy a particular plot of land a Jebusite named Araunah has used as a threshing floor. When David approaches the property owner about the idea, Araunah is all for it. He even offers to give the land to David. David insists on paying, however. He famously tells Araunah, "I will not sacrifice to the Lord my God burnt offerings that cost me nothing."

This place, the threshing floor of Araunah, becomes an important and holy location in Jewish history. The book of 2 Chronicles (3:1) tells us that the site of this altar David built will later become the Temple of Solomon. Formerly it been known as Mt. Moriah, the place where Abraham went to sacrifice Isaac. While the specific locations are disputed today, it's enough for our purposes to note that this threshing floor was a key place for feeding people. This fact would remain true of threshing floors around the world until the shift from animal power to steam power rendered them inefficient. David's real estate deal, and the realization that he acquired a place with a history of both sacrifice and feeding people, is worth tucking away in the back of our minds as we read again the story of the food fight that Elijah wins on another famous mountain, Mt. Carmel, about sixty miles to the north.

The book of 1 Kings picks up the story with David now an old man. The entire first part of this Bible book is about David's son, Solomon, building a temple to the Lord on that famous threshing floor site. By the middle of the book, Solomon is also building altars to other gods and taking wives from anywhere he can find them. He dies and the kingdom gets split up between two leaders named Rehoboam (Solomon's son) and Jeroboam. Jeroboam invents his own hybrid religion in chapter 12 and appoints "all sorts of priests" selected "of his own choosing." Perhaps it should not surprise us that this new religion revolves around golden calves and sacrifices and festivals to feed the calves . . . seemingly to give the worshipers an excuse to party. By the time Elijah makes his appearance in 1 Kings 17, a whole series of really lousy kings have come and gone and the worst guy of all time has taken the throne, King Ahab.

Into this mess comes Elijah, who shows up one day and tells Ahab (my paraphrase), "God sent me here to tell you that it's not going to rain again in Israel unless I say so." In other words, soon there will be no food. This was a direct mockery of Baal, who as the storm god was supposed to bring rain to the earth. Local tradition had it that during times when it did not rain in this semi-arid place, it was because Mot, the god of death, would kill Baal every year, and then Baal's sister Anat would eventually take revenge on Mot and free her brother from death. Whatever the case, Elijah shows up with a claim that he works for a God who presides over all of their territory.

Then Elijah takes off and goes out into the middle of nowhere, to a rugged, desolate place called Kerith Ravine. The word *Kerith* means "cut off," and the prophet indeed is cut off from everything, and the people of Israel are "cut off" from rain. To this barren, isolated place, God dispatches ravens to feed Elijah. Ravens had a reputation of neglecting their own young and refusing to feed them until they grew black feathers, so the fact that these birds would be better at feeding people than Baal was should be heard as a mocking jab at that false god.

Now this is when the story really gets good. After the raven-feeding incident, God tells Elijah to look for his food in another unexpected spot. God chooses a widow in a distant village and sends Elijah to her modest home. When the prophet meets up with this impoverished woman, she seems less than confident in the plan he sets before her. When he asks her for some bread and water, she replies, "I don't even have enough for me and my son. I'm planning to go home right now and cook up what little we have, and then we'll starve. We're not long for this earth." Elijah tells her not to worry about it—to go home and fix him a meal. And, sure enough, every time this widow gives food to God's man, she has more than enough left for herself and her son.

In the following chapter we have what may be the most famous Elijah story—indeed, one of the most famous stories in the Old Testament. Elijah has what I would call a "god-feeding" competition with the prophets of Baal on Mount Carmel. The gist of the competition is a contest to see whose god will respond and cook his own sacrifice on an altar. During the daylong face-off, Elijah teases the prophets of Baal, who resort to cutting themselves and performing all sorts of antics trying to get their god to listen. "Maybe your god's asleep or on vacation, or maybe he's using the john," Elijah hoots at them. "Yell louder and maybe he will come!" But Baal never does show up. In the end, Elijah's God casts consuming fire from on high and burns up everything. So impressive is God's fiery display that nobody on the scene now doubts who the true God is, so Elijah tells the dazzled crowd to slaughter the prophets of Baal.

You'd think Elijah with this sort of access to an arsenal of "air support" in the form of artillery would have the confidence needed to stand against Ahab and Jezebel. Instead, he cuts and runs for his life when Jezebel sends him a nasty, threatening letter telling him what she plans to do to him when she catches him.

The text says, "Elijah was afraid and ran for his life." He runs for a day; and when he gets to the desert, he hunkers down under a tree and prays that he may die. "I have had enough, Lord," he says. "Take my life; I am worthless!" Then he lies down and falls asleep. But an angel wakes him up and says, "Get up and eat!" Elijah looks around, and there by his head is a cake of hot bread and a jar of water. The angel says, "The journey is too much for you." So he eats and the Scripture says that "strengthened by that food, he traveled forty days and forty nights to Horeb."

Where is Horeb? No one knows. It is one of the great mysteries of biblical archeology. Wherever it is geographically, Elijah is back on the same hallowed ground where Moses received the Ten Commandments. Where God appeared in a burning bush. Where Moses struck a rock. He is back where the golden calf was smashed and where the first Passover was celebrated. After this visit by Elijah, it drops out of biblical history and its location fades from the remembrance of God's people.

What's the point of all this? We can tease out of the prophets plenty of themes and meanings and messages that speak powerfully to us today, but the most obvious one to me is this: God will feed you. He is trustworthy. He will show up, he will nourish you, he will provide. The relationship he seeks is not complicated, nor is it based on our merit. It's just a simple process of depending on him.

Like Solomon, you can attempt to build for him the most elaborate, amazing temple, but if you think you are somehow making him happy or feeding his needs, you are mistaken. Like the widow, you may think there is not enough, but if you share in the midst of your own insecurity, he will make sure there is enough for you. Like Ahab, you can worship and depend on the gods of your time and your culture, but they will leave you hungry. Like Elijah, you may want to give up in desperation, but if you look around, God will feed you. Right smack in the middle of nowhere, out of nowhere, he will sustain you so that you can go on. And, just as that original man from Ur tried to feed God by sacrificing his son Isaac at the threshing floor of Araunah, even if we muster up the courage to try, we never can offer sacrifices that match his.

Chapter Fifteen

SILENCE. THEN BREAD FROM HEAVEN

"When people were hungry, Jesus didn't say, 'Now is that political, or social?' He said, 'I feed you.' Because the good news to a hungry person is bread."

—Desmond Tutu

Following the Old Testament is a four-hundred-year gap where things seem to go from bad, to worse, to awful, to unbearable for the Jews. If ever there was a period where the people of God might have doubted whether they served a God who actually loved to feed them, this likely should have been it.

In 332 BC, Jerusalem fell to an obscure historical figure named Alexander the Great, who was on his way to conquer bigger and better towns. About halfway through this Hellenistic/Greek reign, a leader named Antiochus Epiphanes came on the scene. He forced young Jewish boys to undergo reverse circumcisions, flogged an aged priest to death for refusing to eat pig flesh, and butchered a young mother and her seven children for refusing to bow down to an image. He outlawed Jewish religious rites and forced the worship of Zeus. At one point, over the course of three days, he and his army killed forty thousand Jews and sent another forty thousand away into slavery. Finally, this Antiochus invaded the Holy of Holies in the sacred temple and sacrificed a pig to Zeus on the holy altar. Then he smeared the sow's blood everywhere to defile the Jews' holy place of worship. Antiochus wanted to make a point: he wanted the Jews, with all their weird food hang-ups and their ancient, outdated religion, to know that they were no match for him and his crowd. The Jews and their God had met their match.

This event, inflicted on the Jews by an evil ruler known in the prophecies of Daniel as the "abomination of desecration," led to the famous Maccabean Revolt, in which a small guerilla army of Jews fought seven years and eventually regained control of Jerusalem and Judea. The Jewish holiday called Hanukkah celebrates the rededication of the temple and the Maccabean victory over Antiochus.

If Antiochus tried to send the message that he was a no-nonsense guy, the Romans who came after him took it to a whole new level. In the final seventy years leading up to the "common era," the downward spiral of events for the Jewish people seems to go into overdrive. During the thirty or so years from 67 to 37 BC, the Romans waged an increasingly brutal campaign to squash all signs of rebellion. Eventually they sided with a group of Jews with an "if you can't beat 'em, join 'em" mentality and colluded with them to put a partially-Jewish puppet-king on the throne. His name was Herod. During this time, no fewer than one hundred fifty thousand more men perished in Palestine in revolutionary uprisings. In 31 BC an earthquake killed another thirty thousand. It was a catastrophic event that had to leave them wondering if God himself had not shaken the earth as punishment. Finally, around 4 BC, the Romans put their foot down one last time and crucified two thousand Jewish rebels. As Philip Yancey observed about the time leading up to and overlapping with Jesus' lifetime, "Revolt was in the air. Pseudo-messiahs periodically emerged to lead rebellions, only to be crushed in ruthless crackdowns."[1]

In the midst of this mess, during this seemingly hopeless cycle of bad news, destruction, massacre, hunger, and helplessness, something happened that radically changed history. In the obscure, backwater town of Bethlehem (the House of Bread), a baby was born to a peasant girl. This baby was so poor, his family so unconnected, that they slept in a barn in a suburb of Jerusalem during the annual Passover festival. They placed the baby in a feeding trough after he was born. The term for this trough in English, "manger," survives only in the context of references to his birth. In French it survives as a common word, one of the most common, in fact: *manger* means "to eat."

This little baby would grow up and call himself the "Bread of Life." He compared himself to the manna that came down from heaven. He would feed people, break bread with them, and introduce new meaning to the Passover feast by offering his broken body as a final sacrifice. No more feeding God. There had been entirely too many misunderstandings through the years with all the sacrifices—too many adventures in missing the point. The God who loves to feed us showed up and miraculously became the Bread of Life. No more words from a mountain about feasts and festivals. This time "the Word becomes flesh." The God who loves to feed us has broken into history with his final act of nourishment, at the very time when the world is most starved for a Savior.

Note

[1]Philip Yancey, *The Jesus I Never Knew* (Grand Rapids: Zondervan, 1995), 52.

Chapter Sixteen

MAGNIFICAT

"The secret of success in life is to eat what you like and let the food fight it out inside."

—Mark Twain

In 2014 in the journal *Science*, a team of Spanish and Swiss researchers published the results of a sixteen-year-long study of two strange birds. The great spotted cuckoo and the crow have long enjoyed an interesting relationship, to say the least. The spotted cuckoo sneaks in and lays its eggs in the nest of the unsuspecting crow. The crow then raises and feeds the bird's young. This arrangement is a great deal for the cuckoo, but maybe not so great for the crow. At least, that was conventional wisdom for the last fifty years or more.

Conventional wisdom, that is, until recent research turned it all on its ear. The researchers noticed something interesting about nests that contained a cuckoo egg. The crows in nests with cuckoos actually did better—much better, in fact—than those that did not have a cuckoo egg secretly slipped in. At first ornithologists suspected that perhaps the cuckoos had some innate ability to pick winners and lay their eggs in nests of high-performing crow families. Eventually, however, the truth came out. Left to their own devices, the crows had poor outcomes in regard to survival of young, but a crow nest with one of those sneaky cuckoo eggs thrived *because* of that cuckoo. I'll tell you why later.

God pulled off a similar trick two thousand years ago. He snuck a special egg into a very average crow's nest. He chose the nest of Mary and Joseph, and he did not ask if they would feed and raise his son, nor did he consult with them about the shame and problems it would bring them.

As for shame, there was Mary, the teenaged girl, who had to explain the inexplicable to her fiancé. Problems? There was Joseph, who decided to deal with the problem by making plans to "divorce her quietly," as opposed to his first option of exercising his right under the Law to have her stoned. Inconvenience? While it makes for great Christmas cards, being born in an animal barn amid such filth and squalor sounds like a downright dangerous way to deliver an infant. This egg sneaked into their nest seemed to come with a whole heap of trouble.

In the midst of this craziness and before much of the later craziness unfolds, Mary has a song she sings when she meets her pregnant cousin Elizabeth (who is expecting John the Baptist, a man Jesus would later call "the greatest ever born of a woman"). In keeping with our theme of God loving to feed us, this little boy born to Elizabeth would grow up to have a strange diet indeed. Scripture tells us he often ate bugs—locusts, with a little wild honey on the side. Actually "bugs" is a bit too broad. For whatever reason, the Jews could only eat insects with knees. All others, according to Leviticus 11, "were detestable to them."

We call the song Mary sang the "Magnificat," a grandiose-sounding name for a simple and humble little song. I like to imagine that she not only sang it then to Elizabeth, but also at mundane times for years afterward, perhaps while washing dishes and pondering in her heart the meaning of her oldest son—the cuckoo one who had come to her under unexpected and miraculous circumstances.

In the song, Mary mentions the "hungry being filled with good things." Perhaps, if her strength allowed it that night in the Bethlehem stable, she sang it to herself after Jesus was born. If so, the *hungry being filled* line would be particularly apropos. The Bethlehem setting, the manger-feeding trough as a crib, a peasant family too poor to pull strings for a decent room in which to deliver their child, much less buy fancy meals.

Mary's "Magnificat" is one of four hymns that come from a collection of early Jewish-Christian canticles that exude the promise/fulfillment theme of Luke's infancy narrative. Those four songs are Mary's "Magnificat," Zechariah's "Benedictus" (1:68–79), the angels' "Gloria in Excelsis Deo" (2:13–14), and Simeon's "Nunc Dimittis" (2:28–32). Today at Christmas it's hard to turn on the radio and fail to hear one of these four hymns in some form.

The first verse of Mary's hymn pours out praise to God, showing that the problems of God choosing her nest were nothing to her compared to the complete joy of being a part of God's plan. "My soul magnifies the Lord!" she says. Eugene Peterson captures it cleverly in *The Message:*

I'm bursting with God-news;
I'm dancing the song of my Savior God.
God took one good look at me, and look
what happened—
I'm the most fortunate woman on earth!

But she is not content to stop and sing only about how lucky she is herself. She is excited about the changes to come for people like her, the transformation and reversal of the world order to come. The final stanza contrasts three realities of Mary's world as well as three realities of her personal situation: Her lyrics cry out to God that he swap places between the proud and the humble. That the place of the mighty and powerful be reversed with the powerless, and that the rich and well-fed swap places with the hungry.

All of these things happened for Mary and would happen for people who would come into contact with her son Jesus. He humbled the proud, he exalted the powerless, and he took issue with the power brokers at every turn. And he fed the hungry. If not at every chance he had, then certainly a lot. And while his disciples seemed to enjoy it when he humbled the powerful, they often either missed the point or complained when he fed people. We should be careful not to do the same.

Today if we want our lives to be in tune with Mary, it follows that the lyrics of our lives would have a similar theme. Are we concerned about the poor, the powerless, and the hungry? Are we bold enough to embrace spiritual poverty, powerlessness, and hunger in our own lives?

As for the greater spotted cuckoo/crow story we started with, I promised an explanation of why the experts say the crows' nests with cuckoo eggs do so well. The researchers found that the spotted cuckoo emits an odor that keeps predators from their nests. Non-cuckoo nests do not enjoy this hidden protection.

It appears that taking in the abandoned, the unwanted, the smelly, will not only help them. It will save you.

Chapter Seventeen

HUNGER IN THE DESERT

"There is no joy in eating alone."

—The Buddha

If you've never been to the city of Dubai, it's worth the trip. It is home to, at the time of this writing anyway, the world's tallest building in the form of the Burj Khalifa. Towering hundreds of feet above the tallest of Manhattan's skyscrapers, the Burj juts up out of the desert and soars into the heavens. It's an amazing sight, a spectacle in a town of spectacles. My friend Bob Harp, who lived and worked there for an American oil company, likes to say, "Dubai is built by sheiks, but it's not their culture. It's what they think of us. It's a fake city built in the middle of a sandy desert, designed as a place for Westerners and people who like Western stuff to go and do a little shopping." In that regard, Dubai has all the glitz and overdone plasticity of America's own desert town, Las Vegas.

My family had a stopover in Dubai recently on our way back to Uganda, where we lived and worked for nine years as missionaries. We had the good fortune of going in July in the middle of the Islamic fast called Ramadan. I say "good fortune" because it's the slow time of their year when, due to the heat and the holiday, five-star hotels are dirt cheap. The downside of visiting Dubai in July is that it's 110 degrees or more—on a cool day. The other downside of the time we went was that it happened to be Ramadan and everyone was fasting, so you couldn't find food anywhere. If you have ever been on a family vacation and the kids have complained about it, imagine the hottest day you've ever seen, and on that day it is literally illegal to eat. Everyone is sweating, stomachs are growling, and there's no food in sight. Now you have a pretty good idea of what it was like for the Moores and their four kids ages eight to eighteen in Dubai. It was pretty rough.

As we wandered in that stifling desert town, I thought about what it must have been like for Jesus as he fasted for forty days in the desert. It's hot. He's tired. He has not eaten in a month or more. And at just the right time Satan shows up and strikes up a conversation.

"I seem to remember you were born in a feeding trough. Hey, son of the House of Bread! You hungry? You should turn those stones into bread if you are."

If we are to take Scripture at face value, then apparently the devil likes to start with the stomach. The Adam and Eve adventure, at least the misadventure part, starts with the stomach, when Eve chooses to eat forbidden fruit. The Jacob and Esau story involves hunger, temptation, and some short-sighted choices around soup in the kitchen. It should not surprise us, then, that the devil shows up in person to take the lead in launching the first temptation Jesus would face after forty hungry days in the desert. And Satan starts with the stomach. Matthew's Gospel understates for us what all of us already might have guessed. It states simply, "And he was hungry."

Apparently when Satan wants to tempt someone who is in a weakened state, he reaches into his backpack and from somewhere near the top of his bag of tricks he pulls out hunger. In this case it was hunger for bread. "You look empty," he says. "Fill yourself up with these rocks." There are no witnesses. No one will know if Jesus caves. Yet he withstands this challenge by quoting an ancient Scripture from Deuteronomy. "Turn these stones to bread," the devil says. Jesus replies by quoting a centuries-old line from Deuteronomy 8, "Man does not live by bread alone, but by every word that proceeds from the mouth of God" (Matt. 4:4). He pulls this quote from a context in Deuteronomy where the Jews had wandered forty years in the desert. In effect he says to Satan, "Forty years is a lot longer than forty days. I will be faithful."

When he quotes from Deuteronomy 8, Jesus is referring back to Israel's wilderness experience. The full text reads as follows:

> All the commandments that I am commanding you today you shall be careful to do, that you may live and multiply, and go in and possess the land which the LORD swore *to give* to your forefathers. You shall remember all the way which the LORD your God has led you in the wilderness these forty years, that He might humble you, testing you, to know what was in your heart, whether you would keep His commandments or not. He humbled you and let you be hungry, and fed you with manna which you did not know, nor did your fathers know, that He might make you understand that man does not live by bread alone, but man lives by everything that proceeds out of the mouth of the LORD. Your clothing did not wear out on you, nor did your foot swell these forty years. Thus you are to know in your heart that the LORD your God was disciplining you just as a man disciplines his son. Therefore, you shall keep the commandments of the LORD your God, to walk in His ways and to fear Him. (1–6 NASB)

Perhaps Jesus quotes from Deuteronomy 8 in order to point to the similarity between his experience and Israel's experience in the desert wilds. Israel failed this test. Jesus, in taking Israel's place, succeeds.

Others in Scripture had taken and failed this same test. As mentioned above, the temptation of Adam and Eve in the Garden, the one that plunged the whole human race into sin, was this same test of appetite. Jesus' wilderness temptation is the beginning of a test that will win the human race back by succeeding where both Adam and Israel had failed.

The sin linked to appetite was much more than Adam and Eve simply being hungry. The devil tempted them to doubt God and his word. God had warned the garden-dwellers that if they ate the forbidden fruit, they would die. But Satan assured them that this was an empty threat, that God could not be trusted.

"And the serpent said to the woman, [If you eat of this tree], you shall not surely die" (Gen. 3:4). In the next verse Satan tempts them with an even bigger kind of carrot. He seduces them to believe that they can become their own god. "God knows that your eyes will be opened as soon as you eat it, and you will be like God, knowing both good and evil" (NLT).

In the wilderness narrative of Israel's exodus, after escaping from awful lives of slavery in Egypt, the Israelites refuse to trust God for their daily bread. Their appetites get the best of them. They get a little hungry, things get tough, and their religion goes out the window.

In the Jesus' wilderness narrative, Satan is back, tempting Jesus to take care of his own needs, to provide his own food miraculously rather than allowing God to supply his diet needs in God's own time and in God's own way. The devil starts his battle with Jesus with a tried-and-true method that had served him well with humankind in the past. He tempts Christ to doubt his Father's sufficiency, just as he tempted both Adam and the Israelites. They caved and doubted God's sufficiency. Jesus refuses Satan's bait. It's not easy being human. We get hungry every few hours, and that same old temptation to fill ourselves with the wrong stuff is back, and it's as appealing as ever. It's even harder when that hunger shows up while we are going through a wilderness experience. When hunger hits in the wilderness, humans do not have a very good track record of managing the situation well. Yet we serve a God who has an impressive wilderness track record when it comes to nourishing us with the right stuff at the right time.

Pithy advice as to how to emerge from these situations unscathed is easier to pen than to follow. Maybe it's enough to suggest that we could do worse than to do what Jesus did and fall back on the ancient Scripture from Deuteronomy 8: "Man does not live by bread alone, but man lives by everything that proceeds from the mouth of God."

Chapter Eighteen

THE SON OF MAN CAME

"I hated this movie. Hated hated hated hated hated this movie. Hated it. Hated every simpering stupid vacant audience-insulting moment of it. Hated the sensibility that thought anyone would like it. Hated the implied insult to the audience by its belief that anyone would be entertained by it."

—**Roger Ebert**, in his review of Rob Reiner's 1994 movie *North*[1]

Sometimes it's best just to be direct and give our honest opinion about something. No punches pulled, no beating around the bush, no matter how painful. Just the hard truth. I don't pull this off very well or very often. In fact, I tend to be a conflict-avoider extraordinaire. Partly it's conflict avoidance, but mainly it's because I know that most of my "truths" are just my opinions, and I don't want to come off sounding opinionated. We all have subjective, passionate views that sometimes come out strongly stated, though few of us have the guts to state our opinions quite as directly as Ebert spouted his opinion of Rob Reiner's film. Most of us had mothers who taught us to be careful and thoughtful with our opinions, but I find it hard to communicate the truth—real truth—with grace as well. They seem to be on opposite ends of the spectrum, either/or options—either truth or grace—never both at the same time.

Jesus was *full* of grace and truth. As my friend and mentor Dr. Monte Cox likes to say, "He is not half grace and half-truth. He is full of both—simultaneously." To the religious folks around him, Jesus often communicated truth with a hard edge. Nowhere was this truer than in the way he spoke about food and meals and the way he addressed the Jewish cultural and religious rules, regulations, and hang-ups concerning meals.

Meals for Jesus represented something bigger than just refueling. For Jesus, meals were an opportunity to usher in, little by little, a new order, a new way to see who is in and who is out, a new kingdom. In fact, it is not an overstatement to say that Jesus' choice of who he ate with played a big role in getting him killed.

In many ways, the question, "Who can I eat with?" was not "a" question for Jews in Jesus' time. It was "the" question. That's why his enemies criticized him in Luke 15 (and in Mark 2, and Matt. 9) by muttering under their breath and directly asking his disciples, "Who does this guy think he is? Look who he eats with!" It was another way of saying, "Isn't it obvious he's not legit? He either does not know or does not care about the most commonsense, basic, foundational issues of eating *clean* food with *clean* people!" For the Jews of Jesus' day, this was Godliness 101, and if you flunked this basic course or had no interest in it, how could you have anything meaningful to add regarding more advanced issues? Yet in Jesus' case, it was not that he didn't get it. He simply didn't care. He was like Roger Ebert the movie critic saying, "I hate your meal rules. Hate them. Hate hate hate hate hate hate hate them." I'm convinced he hated those rules because, like so many religious rules in both those times and today, they had become an adventure in missing the point. Accordingly, to provide a counterpoint, he offered them a repeated example of eating and drinking with anyone and everyone who would listen.

As I suggested in the Introduction to this book, I find it fascinating to read the book of Luke and look for how many times Jesus is either coming from, or going to, a meal. Go ahead, try it. Grab a Bible, flip it open to Luke (it's a better book on food and meals than this one anyway), and see if you can find a chapter that does not have him involved in some sort of meal. If you take the challenge, you'll find a few, but not many. The meal theme in Luke is remarkable.

In his book *A Meal with Jesus,* Tim Chester asks the reader to complete the statement "the Son of Man came . . ." Scripture gives us three answers. One is in Mark 10:45, where Jesus says he came "to serve, not to be served" and to give his life as a ransom. A second is in Luke 19:10, where Jesus tells us he came "to seek and to save the lost." Both of those, Chester observes, are statements of purpose. *Why* did Jesus come? He came to serve, give, seek, and save. A third Scripture where we find the phrase, "The Son of Man came . . ." is Luke 7:34, where Luke says, "The Son of Man came eating and drinking." This is not a purpose statement but a statement of method. *Why* did Jesus come? He came to seek and save lost people like you and me. With what ethos or attitude did he come? He came with the attitude and the heart of a servant and to serve and not to be served. *How* did Jesus come? What was his method? He came eating and drinking.

Apparently Jesus was pretty good at eating and drinking, because he was criticized for doing too much of it. Indeed, he called the naysayers out on their critique of him when he said, "The Son of Man has come eating and drinking, and you say, 'Look at him! A glutton and a drunkard'" (ESV)! They completely missed the *why* of his presence—that he was there to save them. They missed the *attitude* with which he came, that of a servant. And they missed the *how* as well. They missed the fact that meals were an everyday opportunity to be inclusive and welcoming and not, as they made them, a mandate to be as exclusive as possible.

In Luke 5:33 the Pharisees and their cronies noticed that Jesus had just come from eating at the house of a tax collector, and they attacked him, "The disciples of John and the Pharisees fast . . ., but your disciples go on eating and drinking." To answer this, Jesus told them a short parable about an important aspect of meals, the wine they drank. He talked about wineskins, the containers they used to hold wine. He reminded them of the obvious fact that if an old wineskin had already been stretched to the limit, the expansion of new wine poured into it would rupture the skin, destroying both it and the wine. "My new kingdom ways won't fit into hearts made brittle by your old laws and rules," he was warning them. His kingdom was expanding, and their brittle old kingdom was certainly not about to stretch to accommodate anything new. The two would not do well together. Nowhere was this more evident than in their differing opinions about who should be seated at the dinner table.

Today in our attempts to follow Jesus in our churches, we don't have much of a problem missing either the why or the ethos of the reason that the Son of Man came. Those of us who are evangelicals, whether we like the name or not, have been branded with a name that marks us as seeking and saving the lost. We get that part. We are also enamored with service projects and service language that show that we are at least trying to emulate Jesus as servants. Whether we do a very good job of it or not is up for debate, but nearly every church at least talks about and promotes service opportunities week in and week out.

But, like the Pharisees before us, most of us don't do a very good job of the eating and drinking part. We leave our buildings each week and often participate in contrived and unintentionally demeaning service projects to the "poor" or other target groups. What we should be doing is just buying some poor fellow lunch. Three times a day, every day, we sit down to eat something and, while hopefully most of those times should be spent dining with our families around our own tables, the times when we are not together as families are opportunities to eat with someone who is lonely, with someone who is estranged, with someone who feels "lost" but will never tell anyone or be obvious enough about their problems to be the target of any ministry or service project. We often assume that ministry efforts must be dramatically self-sacrificial or require a lot of spiritual depth and discipline to pull off. But maybe real ministry is just lunch. Maybe it's just eating and drinking. If it is, this lowers the bar to a level where all of us can rise to the challenge. Maybe that's somewhere near the evangelical heart of a God who loves to feed us.

Note

[1]Roger Ebert, *I Hated, Hated, Hated This Movie* (Kansas City: Andrews McMeel, 2000), 261.

Chapter Nineteen

THE IMPOSSIBLE TASK

"Emikwano emitufu gimeneka enswa.
True friendship means you share half a termite for supper."

—Ugandan proverb

Anyone who has ever hosted a big gathering knows that the central concern in the planning process almost always turned out to be, "Will there be enough food?" Whether it's the fairly simple task of ordering enough pizza for a teen event or arranging catering for a more complicated event like a wedding reception. Fortunately, my wife handles such tasks in our family, but when I do, I always panic as the event draws near, and I order way too much. The fear of not having enough grips me, and I overdo it. Every time. I never get it right.

In Luke 9 Jesus hands the disciples an impossible task. They come to him with a huge problem and a solution to that problem. "The people are hungry, Lord," they tell him. "Send them away." The crowd is immense. It numbers in the thousands. Since feeding so many people clearly is an impossible task, Jesus' men already know what has to happen. They just need someone with the authority to do the unpopular job of sending everyone packing. "Let them go to the nearby towns and villages and *get for themselves* something to eat."

How does Jesus reply? He simply tells his men, "You feed them." After what I imagine must have been a long, awkward pause, one of them pipes up to explain their concern. "Lord," he estimates, "it would take eight months' wages to feed so many." The disciples are not geniuses, but they can do the simple math. They are broke, poor (now largely unemployed) fishermen, and the people outnumber them four hundred to one, or more.

It is interesting to note that just a few verses earlier, in Luke 9:3, Jesus had sent them out with the specific instructions, "Don't take any bread." Now he gives them the impossible task of whipping up a meal out of nothing in the middle of nowhere. The message is clear: Jesus' men are responsible for these people, even if all they can see is their inability and insufficiency to care for them. The disciples see this for what it is—a completely impossible and unfair assignment. Jesus is asking them to do something that is beyond their means.

Yet the feeding of the five thousand is one of those rare stories included in all four Gospels. I would suggest that it shows up that often because of how powerfully the point is made to each of the men who are present that day. He gives them an impossible task because he wants them to see clearly that it's not about them, or their ability, or their perceived resources.

"What do you have?" Jesus asks them. They report that they have five loaves of bread and a few fish, and he tells them, "Bring what you have to me." When they come with the five loaves (which, Bible scholars tell us, were about the size of typical European hard rolls), I imagine Jesus looking at those meager pieces of bread, then putting them down on a cloth, doing the math, maybe recounting a few times. And finally saying, "Okay, let's see . . . one, two, three, four, and five. Okay, I think we have it. One per thousand. That should be just about right!"

All of us who have read the Gospels know the end of the story. Everyone gets fed, and one big basket full of bread is left over for each of the apostles. I laugh when I think of the clean-up process, with each of the Twelve left lugging a big, heavy basket full of bread down the hillside. Right back to the spot where they said, "Send them away, Lord."

Jesus did this to prepare them for the next impossible task. Remember his last words to them? "Feed my sheep!" (John 21:15–17). This time it would not be the same sort of bread. This time the impossible task was to proclaim forgiveness, redemption, and reconciliation to a broken and hungry world. More than two billion people later we are still feeding, still feeling underresourced, still tempted to say, "Send them away, Lord," much more quickly than we are to simply take what we have to Jesus.

One particular part of the disciples' response disturbs me most deeply in regard to our churches today. That's when the disciples suggest: ". . . so that they might *buy for themselves* something to eat in the nearby markets." Whose problem is this? The people's problem, Jesus' men imply. It's their fault. They should have brought a lunch. They should have planned better. They should dig into their own pockets and suck it up, get a job, get off welfare, quit being lazy, and solve their own problems. Perhaps I am overreaching, reading something into the text, and laying something on the disciples they don't deserve, but when I hear this same attitude conveyed on the lips of Christians today, I fear it comes more from an American political or cultural ethos than it does from a true biblical or godly mindset.

Welfare has not worked in our country (or in any other) as a solution to hunger and need, because giveaways always promote dependency. No doubt about that. Milton Friedman was right when he said, "There is no such thing as a free lunch." In a way, Jesus agreed, because he was pretty hard on those who showed up at his gatherings looking only to fill their bellies. He called them out on it and made it clear that they were missing the point. But I fear we are often too eager to embrace free-market economic principles and make the right-headedness of those underlying principles the excuse for our complete apathy and lack of interest in God's children who are hungry. We can end up sounding a lot like the original disciples who said, in effect, "This is not our problem. Send them away." "You feed them," Jesus replied calmly. What he was really saying was, "I will feed them. I just want you to be involved by bringing whatever little you have to give. Whatever it is, it will be enough. I will make it enough." The problem today is that free-market economics at its core is based on the basic economic principle of scarcity discussed earlier in Chapters Six and Seven. The disciples in this instance were limited by the myth of scarcity. Jesus, the abundant, nourishing God-man, was not.

This Gospel story raises the question, what about us? Can we reach our communities with the gospel of reconciliation and forgiveness? Can we take our meager five loaves and attempt something audacious? Something impossible? I fear that we are often so obsessed with the (otherwise excellent) aspect of our culture that focuses on planning, self-reliance, and a free-market economic philosophical framework that we would never even attempt anything as audacious as feeding the five thousand. Our modern American churches may not get it, but the early church father, Cyril of Alexandria, certainly did when he said this:

> "There were also gathered twelve baskets of fragments." And what do we infer from this? A plain assurance that hospitality receives a rich recompense from God. . . . Let nothing, therefore, prevent willing people from receiving strangers. . . . Let no one say, "I do not possess suitable means. What I can do is altogether trifling and insufficient for

many." Receive strangers, my beloved. Overcome that reluctance which wins no reward. The Savior will multiply the little you have many times beyond expectation. "Although you give but little, you will receive much. For he that sows blessings shall also reap blessings," according to the blessed Paul's words (2 Corinthians 9:6). . . . We have a responsibility to welcome people to the messianic banquet.[1]

Note

[1]Cyril of Alexandria, *Homily 48, New Testament vol. 3, Ancient Christian Commentary on Scripture: Luke,* ed. Arthur A Just Jr. (Downers Grover, IL: Intervarsity, 2003), 152.

Chapter Twenty

TEACH US TO PRAY/ *EPIOUSIOS*

"Lord, we know that you'll be coming through the line today, so Lord, help us to treat you well. Help us to treat you well."

—Prayer of **Mary Glover**, an African American helping with the weekly food line a mile and a half from the U.S. White House (Quoted by Jim Wallis in *Sojourners*)

As I already have mentioned more than once in these pages, I am fortunate to have started and to now get to run a company called MANA Nutrition. We make little packets of peanut butter for UNICEF and the World Food Program and other products known in the industry as RUTF (Ready to Use Therapeutic Food). Our products are used in the front line of the battle against malnutrition in developing nations. At MANA we are not a faith-based group in that we don't use overtly Christian language or espouse doctrine in any way. We serve all children of all faiths, with no mention or expectation of religion entering into the conversation. We leave that important work for others.

At MANA we have company T-shirts, and on the backs of those shirts between the shoulder blades is a tip-of-the-hat to the faith that compels most of us here to go to work every day. It is the Greek word *epiousios* (ep-e-oo-se-os). We use it as a greeting at times in our company, or more often as a goodbye, sort of like the word "aloha" in Hawaii. What does it mean? Well, no one really knows for sure. But we have a few guesses.

In Luke 11 the disciples come to Jesus and ask him to teach them to pray. As he does, he uses the word *epiousios*. It is the only adjective in the Lord's Prayer, and usually it is translated as "daily bread." Rather than start there, let's end there and look first at the preceding chapters in Luke for clues that might provide a context and help us to see if our food-and-meal theme is alive and well.

We could go farther back in Luke's Gospel, but it will take too long, so for our purpose here let's just go back a few pages to the eighth chapter. In Luke 8 Jesus brings Jairus's daughter back from the dead by saying in verse 54, "My child, get up." The people there are laughing at Jesus for talking to a dead girl, when she stands up, and he immediately says to them, "Give her something to eat." It's sort of a throw-away line, not one in my opinion that necessarily has a lot of deep theological significance. What's interesting to me is that Luke found it memorable enough to include it. Mark's

Gospel, famous for its economy of words and traditionally thought to be influenced by Peter's memories, includes this little line as well. Jesus, at the height of an amazing, miraculous moment, refuses to revel in the "super-spirituality" of the occasion. The laughing has stopped and it gives way to awe as he says, "I bet she's hungry. Go grab her something to eat, will you?"

From those closing lines in Luke 8, we head to the opening lines of the next chapter, where Jesus sends out the twelve apostles. "Take no bread," he tells them. They go out preaching from village to village, and by the time we get to verse 10 they are back with Jesus. Luke tells us that although they attempt to be alone with Jesus, the crowds seek them out. This is where the same guy who just told them, "Take no bread," now tells them to feed five thousand people. We've just dealt with this amazing story, but I think it's safe to say that the memory of this miracle has to be alive and well in the apostles' minds when, not long afterward, they ask him to teach them to pray.

Luke 10 begins with Jesus sending out not just twelve preachers, but this time seventy-two, sent in pairs to "every town and place where he was about to go." In doing so, he uses harvest language and says to them, "The harvest is plentiful," as he gives them instructions about how they should behave in these towns. In verse 5 and following, Jesus says to his delegates, "When you enter a house . . . , if a man of peace is there . . . , stay in that house eating and drinking whatever they give you." There is a lot here to think about, but one thing we should not miss is the centrality of the meals and the eating and drinking. Sure, they have to eat to survive, but these meals appear to be the setting for the unfolding and communication of Jesus' plans soon to come their way. In fact, in his instructions Jesus gets even clearer, "When you enter a town and are welcomed, eat what is set before you . . . and tell them, 'The kingdom of God is near you.'" Jesus imagines, even predicts, that they will be sitting around eating in the villages where they show up as his advance team.

Later in Luke 10 a man approaches Jesus and asks not just "a" question, but what is really "the" question for religious people: "What must I do to inherit eternal life?" Jesus lets the man answer his own question by asking him to quote the Law. The man recites the *Shema*, the Hebrew word for "hear"—the first word in "Hear, O Israel. . . ." The man answers Jesus correctly by quoting the "love the Lord your God" part, and then he ends with the less clear "love your neighbor" part. Then he asks Jesus, "Can you clarify for me who my neighbor is?"

Jesus answers the man's first question by coming back at him with a question. Basically Jesus says, "What do you think?" But in response to the fellow's second query, Christ does not ask the man about his own ideas. Instead, he tells a story that unmasks the typical Pharisaic notion about neighbors and neighborliness. It appears that in this instance Jesus is not really interested in hearing what this guy thinks, possibly because this guy is from a crowd that gets the neighbor question egregiously wrong.

The now-famous Good Samaritan story features a hero with whom the Jews could not even sit down to eat. Not only were the Samaritans outcasts, they were despised enemies of the Jews. In Jesus' telling of the parable, this enemy stops and helps the Jewish man who is in bad shape after getting mugged. He does three things: He gets off his donkey (my dad's King James Version Bible has him getting off another word for donkey), he gets down in the ditch, and he reaches into his own purse to care for the man. The third part of this has the Samaritan taking the man to an inn along the way and striking a deal with the innkeeper. "Take care of this guy. Nurse him back to health." In the Scripture the Samaritan says literally, "Look after him." What did this mean? The Samaritan had already administered medical care by bandaging his wounds and putting oil and wine on them. His instructions and payment to the innkeeper had to include, if not exclusively, then primarily, feeding the guy until he got back his strength.

So, in Jesus' story, the man with whom none of the straightlaced Jews would eat a meal, ends up feeding the Jew in distress. The original question, "What must I do to inherit eternal life?" could really be put another way. It could be stated, "What's the most important thing in the world?" Jesus replies by saying, "Love God and be a true neighbor by bandaging and feeding hungry, hurting people." In the end he looks back at his inquisitor to see if he gets the point, and he asks, "Who was the neighbor to the man in need?" Perhaps unable or unwilling to have the word "Samaritan" pass his lips, the original questioner replies to Jesus, "The one who helped him." Jesus looks back and says, "You should be like him." What does it mean to be like "the good Samaritan"? Focus on life, not death. Make your enemies your neighbors, not your neighbors your enemies. And show people that compassion has no boundaries, because judging people on the basis of their religion or their ethnicity will leave all of us dying in ditches.

Right after the Good Samaritan story, Luke 10 closes at Mary and Martha's house with yet another mealtime story. Martha, who is literally serving God, pauses and says what all of us have said to God at some point, "Don't you care?" If we read Martha's message carefully, we can see a whole lot of "me" and "my" in her words. "Lord, don't you care that *my* sister has left *me* to do all the work by *my*self?" Jesus reminds Martha that being busy and distracted at mealtime is not as useful or impressive as actually sitting and listening to your guests. Especially to the guest they have that particular day. Luke doesn't tell us how Martha took this, but in our culture of fast food and rushed meals, this is a tough one for us to hear today.

All of that context, all those stories around food and eating and meals and nourishing one another, bring us to Luke 11. The disciples ask Jesus to teach them to pray, and he obliges. In doing so, he calls God "Father," a name Abraham, Moses, and David never dared to call their Maker. Then Jesus continues with his prayer lesson by saying: "When you talk to the Father, talk to him about who he is. Say: 'Father, you are great, you are hallowed.' Then talk to him about his program. Say, 'Your kingdom come, your will be done. Do whatever it is you want to do here on Earth. Let your program unfold.' Then talk to him about his provision. Ask for three square meals, no more." Catholics call this, "The fourth petition of the Our Father."

This is where our mystery word, *epiousios* (ἐπιούσιον), appears. Scholars call it a *hapax legomenon*, a word that occurs only once within a context. This word *epiousios* does not appear elsewhere in Scripture, nor can we find it anywhere in other Greek literature. Biblical scholars seeking to derive meaning for a particular word usually can look in extra-biblical literature like Homer's *Iliad* or his *Odyssey* to see how that word was used there. No such luck with this particular word. It does not appear anywhere else in Greek writings.

Epiousios is typically translated in English as "daily," but the Greek term used elsewhere throughout the New Testament for "daily" is *kath hemeran* (καθ' ἡεμέραν), "according to the day." It was translated as *quotidianum* (daily) in the Venus Latina and revised to the more cool-sounding term, *supersubstantialem,* in the Latin version of Scripture known as the Vulgate. Those attending the Council of Trent in 1551 liked the sound of that and associated it with the Eucharist and its "super-substantial bread."

Others have suggested that it actually means "enough for the day" or "enough for tomorrow" or "necessary." Among scholars there is little clarity, so our *hapax legomenon* appears to be an invented word that fills a unique need. Origen, a church father renowned as a master of the Greek language, mentions *epiousios* in his book *On Prayer*. He suggests the word was "formed by the evangelists" perhaps to translate the original Hebrew or Aramaic word that Jesus may have used to teach his disciples. Dante, the medieval poet famous for his *Inferno*, guessed that Jesus actually used the word "manna," and in his *Purgatorio* (Canto 11) Dante translates this part of the Lord's Prayer: "Give us today our daily manna." (As you can imagine, at our company we love Dante for this.)

Whatever the case, our mystery-word *epiousios* seems a bit shortchanged when we translate it simply with the English word "daily." Perhaps when we pray this prayer, we should be imagining the biblical notion of manna, the bread that came down from heaven each day to feed the wandering Jews on their way to the Promised Land. And, at the same time, we should recall Jesus' temptation when he reminds Satan that "man does not live by bread alone, but man lives by everything that proceeds from the mouth of God" (Matt. 4:4; Deut. 8:3). Or maybe we should recall Jesus' miracles involving the feeding of the five thousand, when he calls himself the "Bread of Life" and promises the Eucharist (John 6).

Or perhaps we should try to hear it for the first time as the disciples did that day, in the context of what had just happened in their lives. Can we hear this unusual word in the setting of the Gospel of Luke where Jesus was always headed to or coming from a meal? *Epiousios* in the life of that little girl in Luke 8, who was dead and risen by Jesus. *Epiousios* for the people in the villages, who welcomed and ate with the Twelve and the seventy-two as they brought news that the kingdom of God was upon them. *Epiousios* for the five thousand and the twelve basketfuls left over. *Epiousios* for the injured man in the ditch, who was treated by a stranger who through his swollen eyes probably looked like an enemy who had stopped to finish him off. *Epiousios* for Martha, who was worried and distracted about many things and had a whole lot of "me" at the center of her worries.

Epiousios. Maybe there is enough for today? Maybe there is enough for tomorrow? Certainly there is with the God who loves to feed us.

Chapter Twenty-One

OF FOOLS AND BANQUETS AND LOSTNESS

"Donde come uno, comen dos. Where one eats, two can eat."

—Colombian proverb

The group of Christians who founded America's first colony at Jamestown did so under strange communist principles. Conservative pundits are quick to point out rightly today that this experiment ended in starvation. No doubt the tragic results played a role in the decision of the next governor, Capt. John Smith (the one of Pocahontas fame), to run his colony in a different fashion. He posted a sign in the middle of the public square that said, **"He who does not work shall**

not eat." This was not original, of course. It is a quotation pulled directly from Paul's writings in 2 Thessalonians 3:10. To urge obedience to his new policy, Capt. Smith wrote:

> Countrymen, the long experience of our late miseries I hope is sufficient to persuade everyone to a present correction of himself. And think not that neither my pains nor the adventurers' purses will ever maintain you in idleness and sloth. . . . The greater part must be more industrious, or starve. . . . You must obey this now for a law, that he that will not work shall not eat.

Smith sets forth to his threatened colony what would become a fundamental American premise for those living in any community. "If you won't work, you won't eat." It strikes us as common sense today. It was a pragmatic rule, not a pithy philosophical statement. The starvation that had resulted from their previous communist experiment was a clear sign to Smith that someone needed to put down their foot.

Speaking of communist experiments—Vladimir Lenin also quoted this verse from the writings of Paul and referred to it as a founding principle of his ideology. The phrase appears in his 1917 work, *The State and Revolution*. Through this slogan Lenin explained that in socialist states only productive individuals could be allowed access to the "articles of consumption." He saw it as a necessary principle under socialism, the preliminary phase of the evolution toward a communist society. Later, Article 12 of the 1936 Soviet Constitution stated: "In the USSR work is a duty and a matter of honor for every able-bodied citizen, in accordance with the principle: 'He who does not work, neither shall he eat.'"

They make for strange bedfellows, Lenin and Smith, and though their experiments in community ended up on wildly divergent paths, it appears that they started in the same place on the subject of how best to fight off hunger. Namely, "If you're going to eat, you better work for it." Or, as I quoted in earlier chapters from economist Milton Friedman: "There's no such thing as a free lunch."

It is perhaps this Lenin-Friedman-Smith-Pauline worldview that explains why Christians in the United States seem so untroubled by hunger in our world today. No one could claim by looking at either our church budgets or the sermons we preach that addressing hunger on our globe is very high on our agenda. I tend to think this is true, not because we don't care, but because we suspend our sympathy, partly due to assumptions about how industrious these people are. We may not actually say it, but either consciously or subconsciously we tend to think that being hungry and being lazy are connected.

While Paul, Smith, Lenin, and Friedman were right in insisting that we need to work for our food, the facts show that the vast majority of the hungry people in our world are not lazy at all. They are caught in circumstances—trapped, if you will—by a host of largely unrelated happenstance: bad governments, bad weather, bad neighbors, and bad luck dealt to them by the geographical birth lottery.

Those of us who look to Jesus for clues on how to behave in certain circumstances often have to infer what he may or may not have done in a modern world that offers scenarios completely foreign to the world of the Bible. We don't need to guess in the case of hunger, however, since Jesus experienced hunger, spoke about hunger, and dealt with large groups of hungry people on multiple occasions. In fact, if we are to take Luke's Gospel seriously, it appears that Jesus wove a hunger/food theme into much of his preaching and his parables.

Nowhere is this starker than in the chapters in Luke that follow his teaching on the Lord's Prayer. Coming on the heels of the Lord's Prayer and Jesus' talk about daily bread, Jesus jumps right into examples of the extravagant goodness of God. In doing so, all of his examples are food-themed. He talks in Luke 11 about bread, fish, and eggs. In verses 5–8 he tells a story about a guy who pesters his neighbor for bread, the message being: if you are a good, though reluctant, neighbor, God is better. Then Jesus tells another quick story after asking, "If your son asked for fish or an egg to eat, would you give him a snake or a scorpion?" Jesus' message: if you are a good but undemonstrative father, God is better. Coming right after Jesus teaches them to pray, the message is clear: "All you need to do is ask. God will deliver."

In chapter 12, Luke brings us some of Jesus' toughest words, as he warns listeners about wealth. Jesus has a lot to say about wealth in the coming chapters of Luke's Gospel, perhaps because Luke knows it's the number-one threat his Gentile readers will face to their faith. In an agricultural-based economy, wealth and food production are closely linked. In Luke 12:16 we meet a rich man with a problem. He has way too much food. He has just the opposite problem that Capt.

John Smith and the early colonists faced; he has more than he can eat, and more than he can even store.

The text says, "The ground of a certain rich man produced a good crop." Notice, Jesus does not say, "The brilliant agricultural techniques or the hard work of a certain rich man produced the crop." He says "the ground" did it. And it apparently never occurs to this rich man, "Wow! I have more than I need. I should give away what the ground gave me."

Instead, this rich fellow has what to us sounds like a normal thought. He says, "I need a bigger place to put all this food. I will build bigger barns and there I will store all my grain." The next verse is important as well, because it shows that his aspirations and dreams for this bounty really extend no farther than himself. "You have plenty of good things laid up for many years. Take it easy. Eat, drink, and be merry."

This is where the man's name changes from the title that he had for himself—rich, brilliant, planner—to God's name for him: Fool. "You fool!" the Lord says to him. "This very night your life will be demanded from you." The story ends abruptly, coldly, and sadly. The word "fool" seems to echo and reverberate and haunt the pages still today. Luke then takes us directly to Jesus speaking with his disciples. He says to them, "Therefore, I tell you . . . ." And what does he tell them? Don't worry about what you will eat. Life is more than food. Don't worry about barns the way that rich fool did. Birds eat and they don't have barns. God takes care of them.

Then in verse 29 Jesus reiterates, "Do not set your hearts on what you will eat and drink. Do not worry about it. For the pagan world runs after such things." Wow!

About a chapter later, in Luke 14, we find Jesus eating in the home of a Pharisee. For any of us who are tired of dealing with those we perceive to be Pharisees in our lives and in our churches (present and past), it's important to note that Jesus did not give up on them. He expected them to expand their worldview and include others, but apparently, even if they didn't, he was still willing to eat with them.

As the scene opens in this bigwig Pharisee's home, an awkward, uninvited guest shows up at the banquet. The man is suffering from dropsy, which would make him unclean and unfit for the guest list at a dinner at this prominent Pharisee's house. Jesus knows the man needs to be healed more than he needs a meal, so he heals him, thereby breaking a precious Sabbath rule right before their eyes. He asks them if they think it is okay to make sick people well on the Sabbath, and no one ventures an answer. They just sit there quiet. The healed guy leaves, but Jesus keeps him and his kind as the main topic of discussion for the rest of that banquet.

While Jesus is eating in this particular banquet, he watches some people who see eating and banquets as an opportunity to improve their social status. As they come in, they claim the best seats for themselves. Christ uses this as an opportunity to give them a vision of what a real feast in the true kingdom of God would look like. He looks at his host and says, "When you give a luncheon or a dinner, don't just invite your friends and rich neighbors who invited you last week or who might feel obligated to invite you next week. Invite the poor, the crippled, the lame, the blind." In other words, invite unclean people like the guy who just awkwardly walked out of here a few minutes ago after being healed on the Sabbath.

A guest sitting at the table tries to spiritualize Jesus' comment or perhaps show off that he "gets it" and understands the rabbi's comment more than others might. The man alludes to Isaiah 25:6, where the prophet envisions a great messianic banquet, an event long expected by the Jews: "Blessed is the man who will eat at the feast in the kingdom of God."

Jesus seizes the comment but takes it in an unexpected direction by telling another parable. He crafts a story featuring his friend who left earlier, but it is actually a parable about those currently sitting at the table with him, though it's not clear if they understand this. He tells about a guy who prepares a great banquet that is lavish and generous, but none of his invited guests can find time to come. They are full of flimsy excuses and turn him down on the offer to sit down for a meal. "I just got married, I just bought land, I got a new ox." The banquet-giver is angered by their decisions to give their attention to lesser things than to his generous offer, so he repeals the invitation.

He then sends his servants out to invite the poor and the lame and the blind. And when they don't fill all the seats, he extends the invitation to wayfarers on far-off country roads. His intention is to fill the banquet hall so that none of the original invited guests can show up late and claim a seat or get a bite of food. They missed their invitation, and the banquet-giver is through with them.

Though the banquet language is symbolic, Jesus is trying hard to get a not-too-veiled point across to his Jewish hearers.

Namely: You are so hung up on who is in and who is out. Who is clean and who is not. Who is fit for your parties and who is not. You are missing the boat. You eat, but you are starving. You talk a good game, but you are about to get uninvited to the great banquet Isaiah talked about. You are sitting at a banquet *right now*—and missing the God who loves to feed you.

From that scene, Luke takes us to one my favorite chapters in the Bible, Luke 15. In it, Luke records three of Jesus' most famous stories about what I call "lostness"—the lost sheep, the lost coin, and the lost son. While I have read this chapter many times, what I had not noticed for a long time was the occasion in Luke that leads to the telling of these three powerful stories. Luke says, "Now the tax collectors and sinners were all drawing near to hear him. And the Pharisees and the scribes grumbled, saying, 'This man receives sinners and eats with them'" (1–2 ESV). They have completely missed the point of his "Great Banquet" parable from the previous chapter and are still focused on the fact that he does not even try to comply with their eating rules.

Since they are so concerned about who he eats and parties with, Jesus tells them three quick stories. All three of the parables in Luke 15 speak of the tax collectors and sinners—the unclean crowd Jesus seems way too comfortable laughing it up with at parties. They are like the lost sheep, the lost coin, the lost son that Jesus has come to rescue. What is interesting in our immediate quest is what an integral role food plays in at least two of these stories.

The ratios change in the three stories but the point does not. He starts with sheep, something the person in the story has a lot of. He has a hundred sheep and he loses just one. One one-hundredth. Just one percent. The next story is about coins, and the person in this story has just ten. She loses one. One-tenth. Ten percent. The final story is about sons. This father has two. He loses one of them. One-half. Fifty percent.

As city-dwelling Americans, we tend to see these sheep as pets, which they weren't. They were not cuddled or petted. They were food. They were little 401k's. They were a living, breathing, walking repository of wealth for their owner. They would be sold, butchered, roasted, sheared at his discretion, and with the same sort of emotion we have when we scan our debit cards or pull a one-hundred-dollar bill out of our wallets. These sheep were food, either for the current owner or for someone else. Indeed, they were more than food, but they were certainly not pets. They were not mistreated, because they were valuable and useful.

In the story, the shepherd loses one one-hundredth of his means for feeding and caring for his family, so he goes and looks for it.

In the second story Jesus talks of coins, and it's a woman who owns them. She only has ten, and in one careless moment she has misplaced ten percent of what she has. That's a big loss. For someone in those days, it could mean the difference in survival, in eating or not eating. The stakes are higher for her than for the sheep owner. She is serious about finding that coin and seriously happy when she does.

In the final story about the lost son, the stakes are higher still. Not just because he has lost half of something, but because he has lost not a sheep, not a coin, but a son! To lose one son of a hundred would be bad. To lose one of ten would be awful. To lose one of only two would be devastating.

In this story it is food that represents the wayward son's recovery and restoration. But it also vividly represents the rock-bottom reality of his lostness. How lost does a Jewish boy from a good home have to be to "long to fill his stomach with the food the pigs ate"? My language teacher in Africa, Ali Bashir, remains one of my closest friends from my nine years in Uganda. Obviously by his name, Ali is Muslim. We spent so many long hours together learning language that we became very close, and eventually I started treating him as I would any friend. I started playing tricks on him. "How'd you like that ham sandwich I snuck into your lunch yesterday?" He never thought these jokes were funny. In fact, far from laughing, he responded in horror until I assured him it was just a bad joke. Soon I stopped those poor attempts at humor, as I realized that for those whose religion involves food that has been banned by God, dietary restrictions are serious business. Ali, though he felt comfortable in our home, was quite careful about what he ate at our table, and he was also fanatical about washing his hands.

Ali is laid-back compared to the hard-line Muslims of today or the Jews of Jesus' day. I can almost see the Pharisees recoiling, even feeling a little sick at their stomachs because of the lurid example Jesus extemporaneously pulls out of his hat. Eating pig food? Really? That's pretty hungry. That's an extreme example of how low and lost this poor boy is. His lostness, his hunger, and his distance from his father are all one issue.

He "longed for the pig food," but Luke coldly tells us that "no one gave him anything." What a stark contrast to his generous father. As we saw in the bigger-barns story, the hoarders are not generously looking around for those they can bless with their extra food. They are busy building bigger granaries, bigger piggeries. Those starving before their eyes, working in their fields, shoveling slop to their pigs, are invisible.

At this point Jesus continues with the eating-and-drinking theme his enemies introduced with their accusation against him in Luke 15:2. He puts bread-and-hunger language in the boy's mouth as the prodigal recalls longingly how the servants at his father's house are not treated like the servants in this pagan land. The underclass is not invisible to his father; in his economy they have "more than enough bread," while this young rebel is about to "perish here with hunger."

When the lost son finally comes to his senses, he decides to swallow his pride and head home. On the way he practices a speech that goes something like this: "Father, I have blown it as a son. So I am not asking you to give me anything. Just make me one of your servants." His arrogant "father, give me" attitude has disappeared, now transformed by hunger and desperation into a "father, make me" attitude.

When he gets close to home, he starts the speech, but his dad will have none of it. "Let's have a feast!" the father who loves to feed him cries. "Bring me a calf! Let's have a party! Let's celebrate. My son is back, and he's hungry! That's all I ever wanted. For him to realize that his father would love to feed him."

In their book *Misreading Scripture with Western Eyes*, authors Randolph Richards and Brandon O'Brien tell of asking one hundred students in the United States to read the story of the prodigal son and then retell the story as accurately as they could. As they recounted the story, only six of the one hundred students remembered that the prodigal decided to return home after experiencing a famine in a faraway land.

They then conducted the same experiment in Russia, and out of fifty Russian readers, forty-two of them mentioned the famine. The Russian readers saw the famine as an important detail to the meaning of the story, while American readers saw a story about a God who loves us no matter how much we've sinned or strayed away. The Russians, with a cultural history of famine in World War II still deeply embedded in their collective consciousness, saw a story about a God who loves to feed us. The Americans missed it.

Chapter Twenty-Two

FOOD QUESTIONS AT THE WELL

"Olugenda enjala teludda. A visitor who leaves with an empty stomach because you did not offer food will not easily return."

—Ugandan proverb

In John 4 the disciples go to town to buy some food and leave Jesus behind. In my Bible, the line about the disciples going to town to buy food is in parentheses. It seems like a throwaway line, not really needed for the story but just tossed in there for no particular reason. We'll see at the end of the story that this is an important fact that provides context for the entire story. For now, it's enough to know that it was high noon on a hot day, and Jesus, tired from traveling, chooses both a classic and sensible rest stop—Jacob's well outside the town of Sychar.

While his men are gone, not only does he engage in the longest one-on-one chat recorded in Scripture, but he has this long conversation with the most unlikely of characters. An unnamed woman appears at the well with clay jar in hand, and Jesus makes a simple request: "Will you give me a drink?" Shocked that he even dared to speak to her, the woman initially ignores his question. Instead she asks him a question about the rules of engagement. "You are a Jew," she reminds him, "and I am a Samaritan woman. How can you ask me for a drink?"

Jesus has broken every rule in the book to initiate this conversation. First off, Jews were not supposed to speak to Samaritans. Secondly, a reputable rabbi had no business speaking to a shady lady such as this one. And finally, as is true even to this day in orthodox Jewish and Muslim environments, men were not permitted to address women without their husbands around. Everything about this awkward conversation is wrong, and the woman feels it.

It is easy for us to miss much of this due to our lack of awareness of the historical context. Any reader familiar with the story and the social mores of that age would have understood. John feels no need to remind his readers of the obvious. He just assumes we know the background. In short, back in the days of Hoshea, the Samaritans had abandoned the faith. Scripture says, "They followed worthless idols and themselves became worthless" (2 Kings 17:15b). The region fell into the hands of Assyria, and the Assyrian king brought in people from various regions to occupy Samaria. They, as one might expect, brought their own gods and built shrines for them (2 Kings 17:24, 29–31). Intermarried with these pagans, the Samaritans began worshiping the false gods, and drifted farther and farther from the one true God, Yahweh. The woman Jesus is talking to at the well is one of these Samaritans.

Jesus responds to her "Why are you talking to me?" question by saying, "If you knew who I was, you'd ask me for living water." This leads to a back-and-forth conversation that ranges from their mutual grandfather Jacob to deeply personal observations (by Jesus) about the woman's personal life. Once she can see that she has happened upon a very special prophetic rabbi, she asks an important theological question: "Our fathers worshiped on this mountain, and you Jews say that Jerusalem is the place where people ought to worship. What do you think?" (4:20).

She asks this because when the Jews and Samaritans went their separate ways, they established their own worship centers. The sacred mountain worship center for the Jews was Mount Zion, while the sacred mountain for the Samaritans was Mount Gerizim. If the Jews and Samaritans were to patch up their differences, someone would have to give in and come over to the other place of worship. Her logic follows our typical logic when we get into doctrinal disputes with others. We tend to assume that one of us is right and the other is wrong, don't we?

We may do well when we find ourselves at theological odds with our neighbors to employ some of her language. She said, "The well is deep and you have nothing with which to draw." What if we said that to people when confronted with tough questions we know will not be answered or settled? What if we also said, "You know, that well is deep, and I have nothing with which to draw"? Such a response might actually allow us to have a conversation with that person about living water, rather than ending the conversation by showing the person how superior, scriptural, or godly our stance on a given issue may be.

Since Jesus does not clearly blast her for being on the wrong side, the woman seeks some clarity. Basically she says, "Are you asking me to abandon the faith of my fathers and come over to Mount Zion?" At this point we'd expect Jesus to say, "Yes. That's exactly what you should do." But, instead, he says,

> Woman, believe Me, the hour is coming when you will neither on this mountain, nor in Jerusalem, worship the Father. You worship what you do not know; we know what we worship, for salvation is of the Jews. But the hour is coming, and now is, when the true worshipers will worship the Father in spirit and truth; for the Father is seeking such to worship Him. God *is* spirit, and those who worship Him must worship in spirit and truth. (John 4:21–24 NKJV)

Not only is Jesus not interested in following the traditional rules that would have made this conversation impossible from the start, he is also uninterested in her efforts to turn it into a theological question-answer time to establish who was right and who was wrong. He was right and she was wrong about the age-old mountain worship debate. It was a very big and important question, but he did not care about winning the debate. He cared about her seeing who he was and recognizing him as the Messiah.

When the disciples return, they are disturbed to find him talking to the woman, but none of them have the guts to say anything to his face about it. The woman leaves, and they insist that he eat some of the food that they went to so much trouble to procure and prepare. When they offer it, he says, "I have food that you know nothing about."

When I think of the next line as it must have appeared to the author, John, who was a firsthand witness to this event, it strikes me as very funny. John tells us that the disciples began asking each other, "Did someone else go get him some food?" I feel as if John wants to insert here, "We didn't understand Jesus at all. We were so confused. We had spent all this time going after food, and here he was telling us that he already had a secret stash of groceries. We were tired, had walked for miles, and we were half angry and half confused at the whole situation."

Jesus then explains to his men, "My food is to do the will of the One who sent me and to finish that work." In other words, the thing that nourishes me, keeps me strong, and makes me alive, says the God-man to the men, is to do God's will. Not to keep religious rules. Not to perpetuate tradition. Not to keep my foot on the neck of the enemy like that woman you were so disgusted to see me talking with. Not to just live day to day and meal to meal. But to do God's will.

He then speaks to them not of single-meal type food, but of harvests and sowing and long-term, eternal plans to nourish everyone. The story closes in John's Gospel with the heading, "Many Samaritans Believe." Droves of Samaritan people come to believe in Jesus, and later they tell the woman, "We don't just believe because of your testimony but because we have heard ourselves and know that this man is the Savior of the world."

Today, centuries later, even though history does not even record her name, this famous-yet-anonymous woman's story about living water resonates with us powerfully. Those of us who can relate to her—the broken, the sinful, the outsiders, the religiously confused—take heart in her story. Hopefully, like her, we will run and tell others about "the man who told us everything we ever did."

Chapter Twenty-Three

I AM THE BREAD OF LIFE

"Food for one person is enough for two,
that for two is enough for four,
that for four is enough for eight."

—Islamic saying

In the late '50s, at the height of the Cold War, the Americans and the Soviets agreed to hold a cultural exchange to promote understanding between the two sides. After the death of Joseph Stalin in the early '50s, Soviet leader Nikita Khrushchev spearheaded a push to catch and overtake the United States. One of Khrushchev's ideas was this joint cultural exchange with the United States. The Soviets went first. In 1958 they sent their cultural exhibit to be viewed by the

American public in New York City. The United States followed up in 1959 by sending a similar exhibit to the USSR.

In this cultural exchange with the Russians, in addition to other aspects, each side built "model homes" to be displayed in prominent public places in the other's country. The Soviet version highlighted communal living and was displayed in the New York Coliseum and showcased Russian Sputnik satellites, an atomic icebreaker, and simple examples of communal living. The U.S. version sent to be displayed in Moscow focused on our lifestyle, including American jazz, basketball, and even high-heeled shoes. One centerpiece of the exhibit was a model home that featured a modern kitchen that "every American housewife" supposedly could afford.

When Vice President Richard Nixon arrived to open the pavilion in Moscow, he and Soviet Premier Nikita Khrushchev made an unscheduled stop at the Betty Crocker kitchen and engaged in an exchange that became known as the "Kitchen Debate." There at the height of the Cold War with atomic threats looming, and with political, technological, and economic superiority on the line, the two world leaders stood in a kitchen talking about food and how people eat. It was as if each side wanted to say, "Sure you have spaceships and high-tech nuclear devices, but you don't enjoy your food like we do!" At one point, upon seeing all the "labor-saving devices" available to the American housewife, Khrushchev poked fun at Nixon and quipped, "Do you also have a machine that puts food into the mouth and pushes it down?"

In reality both countries were experiencing a cultural upheaval around food, and neither of them was necessarily good. The individualistic, American presentation of "kitchen" and food was defined by technology and a "faster is better" mentality. In the United States, a post-war economic boom that valued individual freedom, efficiency, and materialism had begun to uproot and replace the beauty of a simple meal. On the Soviet side, people often huddled in hallways and corridors of tenements eating lonely, largely tasteless meals. Both sides were hungry for something more than food, one with plenty of freedom but little community; the other with little freedom and forced community.

Khrushchev's attempt at being clever hit close to home because it was only a slight exaggeration. We had a gadget for everything, and this changed the way we lived. More specifically, it changed the way we ate, cooked, and dined. While we did not see it at the time, it turns out that this period in American history saw a shift where Americans, like their Russian enemies, retreated to lonely places to eat. Curtains drawn, TV on, neighbors increasingly excluded, Americans began to eat alone. While the '50s media still portrayed the Norman Rockwell pictures of the joyous American dinner table, such family gatherings would all but disappear from American life in the decades to follow. They gave way to "progress" . . . first TV dinners, then drive-ins, then fast food, then drive-thrus. American eating habits, cooking habits, food production, and nutrition radically changed. By the first decade of the next century, urban guerilla gardener Ron Finley would famously say in a TED Talk, "I'm from Los Angeles, where the drive-thrus are killing more people than the drive-bys."

While we are now able to reflect on the downside of our culture's way of feeding ourselves, we should note that few Russian families experienced the very best of communism around a common table. In their scheme, ten families shared a home with one kitchen and a "common pot," with only four burners for ten families sharing a single spartan stove. A brilliant 2014 National Public Radio piece interviewed Russian social scientists and expert historians, and each spoke of how this scheme backfired. In short, while it was portrayed otherwise by the Soviet regime, there was often distrust and paranoia, and many people came to see the kitchen as a place where a KGB agent could listen in on your life and thoughts, etc. People soon had pots and cupboards with locks on them and increasingly they dispensed with the traditional Russian cultural meal eaten together. Instead, they retreated to eat by themselves in lonely hallways where they often ate simple, flavorless stew because of their poverty. The kitchens were not joyous gathering places around food, as they had been before in idyllic recollections of times past. Now they were quiet, stoic places.

And so, in many ways on both sides of the Cold War, people lacked community around food. While the reasons for this varied, it's no stretch to observe that this was at least partly because each tended to pursue nourishment in ways that did not resonate with God's view of nourishment. On the Russian side, it was more overt and could be traced to the intentional, mandated godless ideology. That ideology proved bankrupt in the end, and to this day the Russian Orthodox Church stubbornly survives. On the U.S. side, an ideology that worshiped individual freedom, efficiency, and materialism took its toll as well. Turns out that it wasn't the nuclear warheads and missiles after all that would offer the biggest threats to both cultures and their welfare. It was something much more subtle that would kill and alienate millions. Food and hunger.

Jesus knew this long before the Cold War, and he offered the solution in his sermon in John 6. In verse 35 Jesus offers one of his famous seven "I am" statements. In each instance he combines those "I am's" with tremendous, powerful metaphors which express his saving relationship vis-à-vis the world. All of those appear in the Gospel of John.

In John's sixth chapter, Jesus as a leader has problems similar to what more recent leaders like Khrushchev and Nixon encountered. He has a bunch of people who need to be fed. So he feeds them. Jesus' feeding program here is plagued by the same problem that dogs modern welfare and food-aid attempts. People eat and are happy, but they get hungry again just a few hours later. Giving them food for free solves a short-term problem but creates a longer-term problem—dependency. In John 6:27, seeing that the crowd is only following him in search of the next free meal, he gets tough on them and accuses them of ignoring his miraculous signs and focusing instead on the free food. He tells them, "Do not labor for food that perishes, but for food that endures to eternal life."

He says this because they are so enthralled with the free food that they are missing out on the fact that their Messiah has come and is in their midst. They follow by asking Jesus for a sign that he really has been sent by God. Apparently his walking across the water and his miraculous feeding aren't sufficient. They remind Jesus that God gave their ancestors manna during their desert wandering. Jesus responds by informing them that they would be better off asking for the true bread from heaven that gives life. When they ask him for this bread, he surprises them with his announcement: "I am the bread of life; whoever comes to me shall not hunger, and whoever believes in me shall never thirst" (ESV).

If you think about it, this is really an amazing statement. By equating himself with bread, the staple food of their culture, he is telling them that he is essential for life. The life he is referring to here is not normal, everyday breathing life, but eternal life. Jesus is trying to do what good preachers do—to move them from thinking and focusing on the physical realm and into the spiritual realm. To do so, he contrasts what he offers as their Messiah with the bread that he miraculously whipped up for them out of nowhere the day before. The bread they thought was miraculous was actually the physical bread that perishes. He, whom they see standing before them appearing as a normal man, is the spiritual bread that brings eternal life.

Probably the most important thing to note in this "I am" statement is that, in saying it, Jesus is making a powerful claim to his audience. This statement is the first of the "I am" statements in John's Gospel. As we see in the Older Testament, the phrase "I am" is the covenant name of God (Yahweh), first used with Moses at the burning bush in Exodus 3:14. It refers to a self-sufficient existence (the theological term for this is "aseity"), an attribute that is impossible for humans but inherent to God. It is also a classic term pulled straight from Scripture and, as such, the Jews listening would have understood it as a claim to deity.

Finally, and most useful for our purposes just now, there are the familiar words "hunger and thirst." It's obvious here that Jesus is not talking about alleviating physical hunger and thirst. He is bringing back a phrase that he used in his Sermon on the Mount in Matthew 5. There he says, "Blessed are those who hunger and thirst for righteousness, for they shall be satisfied." So here in John, when he says those who come to him will never hunger and those who believe in him will never thirst, he is letting them (and us) know that he will satisfy our hunger and thirst to be whole, put-together humans. Or to put it in religious language, to be made righteous in the sight of God.

Perhaps those listening that day were like us today, either mired in past regrets or anxious about future fears. Here, as he evokes the very name of God, we have Jesus in the present tense. Not an "I was," not an "I will be," but an "I am." The more we can understand and employ God's "I am" statements in both the Old and New Testaments, the more apt we are to actually experience and realize the peace and joy he intends for us. He reminds them and us of God's call to be present and to live in the present. If we do this, we are free to live and serve and know God today, right now, this hour, this minute, this second—in the present tense. Jesus in the present tense. *I am* the bread of life. It's either bad grammar or a strange and powerful truth.

Chapter Twenty-Four

EAT MY FLESH AND DRINK MY BLOOD

"My doctor told me I had to stop throwing intimate dinners for four unless there are three other people."

—Orson Welles

Few things strike us as being weird more than cannibalism. I wonder if one day soon in our increasingly inclusive society a time is coming when we will openly welcome cannibals into our midst. Can you imagine progressive voices in the media saying, "Listen, fifty years ago we discriminated against people for all sorts of reasons, but now we understand that diversity is a good thing. So if your neighbor wants to eat other people, you should not criticize him or limit his right to free expression of this aspect of his personality."

Ha! Sounds ridiculous now, but maybe we are headed there. I hope not, but to be honest I really can't explain to you why I hope that. What are my biases against cannibalism? It's gross? That's subjective really. It's morally wrong? Says who? It's unhealthy or bad for the human tribe? Where's the science on that, and who's to say it won't help cull the herd? Who knows? Maybe someday soon we will have street vendors with chunks of human meat barbequing them up for people to eat as they stroll the streets or to munch casually in baseball parks.

If that last paragraph made you queasy or a little worried about how disturbed I might be to write it or even to imagine it, then good. You are feeling a tinge of the shock and awe that I believe the original audience felt in John 6 when Jesus told them to eat his flesh and drink his blood. In fact, you are probably not feeling even a hint of the horror they felt, because you (likely) are not Jewish and do not have centuries of food and diet hang-ups and limitations in your family. Jews and Muslims today have all sorts of rules about food—who cooked it and how it was cooked, etc.—that we modern Christians cannot begin to understand. The crowd Jesus addressed would have lived lifetimes filled with concern, anxiety, and preparation regarding this topic, and accordingly, his call for them to eat human flesh and drink human blood would have been utterly offensive and ridiculous to them.

Sociologists and economists tell us that as societies progress economically, they eat more meat. If you are an American reading this book, congratulations. You eat more meat than almost anyone on earth. We eat about ten times more meat than the average person in Mozambique. Why? According to the International Food Policy Research Institute, all countries eat more meat when their incomes grow and they have the economic wherewithal to purchase it. The pattern is so consistent that economists now consider it virtually a law of human behavior. It is as if it is a preference that people are born with. You can go back and reread that if you wish, but the answer to the "why" that I offered above is simply, "Because they do." People eat meat, and when they get more money, they eat more meat.

In addition to this proclivity we humans seem to have to eat meat, it's also interesting to note that ceremony is often attached to the eating of meat. If you don't believe it, check out American males when they barbeque. Anyone who has a friend with a Big Green Egg knows this. Macho American men see the barbeque as their territory. The kitchen? No way. The grill, and the opportunity to play with fire and cook some animal flesh? You bet! Like us, other cultures from the ancient Jews to the Polynesians to Native Americans all have distinct ceremonies and rituals around the grilling and eating of meat.

A vegetarian reader at this point would likely be quick to point out that this love affair we have with eating meat—especially red meat—is not good for us. Both science and the medical community are on their side as well, but we are notoriously slow to listen to either science or doctors when it comes to things like health. Truth be told, our consumption of red meat peaked back in the 1970s, and chicken slowly started to become king. This turned out to be bad news for the chickens but good news for our coronary arteries.

Given our fascination with meat eating, it is safe to say that no other culture in history has as much experience with eating flesh as we do. You name it, we'll eat it—pigs, goats, cows, fish, even alligators and snakes! Yet eating human flesh to us is crazy. Unthinkable. Disgusting. Gross. Criminal. How much more so would it be for a culture of people with a long list of dietary restrictions surrounding the killing, preparation, and consumption of animals.

In regard to the context of Jesus' words in John 6, it's important to remember here that the day just before Jesus says this, he had fed five thousand people with just a few loaves and fish. He then sent his men away in the only boat available, so the next morning when people encounter Jesus in Capernaum, they know he got across the lake miraculously. If he is looking to launch his political career, this is the time. The people are clamoring to make him king. So he gathers his adoring fans and begins what seems like an assault on what he knows to be a misplaced passion for him to usher in change as the head honcho.

First, he talks about their appetites.

> Jesus answered, "Very truly I tell you, you are looking for me, not because you saw the signs I performed but because you ate the loaves and had your fill. Do not work for food that spoils, but for food that endures to eternal life, which the Son of Man

> will give you. For on him God the Father has placed his seal of approval." (John 6:26–27)

Notice that Jesus begins by slapping down their misplaced appetites, warning that they were getting "filled up" and satisfied with the wrong sort of food. But he is also careful not to bash their hunger for food; he just wants to reorient them to the right food. "Don't go looking for normal food that will spoil, but instead you should look for eternal food." Then he makes a promise to them by describing that diet as food "which the Son of man will give to you." Here Jesus lets them know that seeking after what he gives, after the blessings he provides, is not the same as believing in him and trusting him. It is a message we would do well to internalize today.

To test them even further, he begins to make some statements that sound strange indeed. He tells them that the true bread that comes down from heaven will allow them to live forever. Then he pushes it to the max and says:

> Very truly I tell you, unless you eat the flesh of the Son of Man and drink his blood, you have no life in you. Whoever eats my flesh and drinks my blood has eternal life, and I will raise them up at the last day. (John 6:53–54)

Suddenly the "Jesus for King" campaign evaporates. The crowd disperses, mumbling to themselves, "This guy is nuts! He wants us to eat his flesh and drink his blood!" They missed his point, and likely no one put two and two together and got the point until after his death, burial, and resurrection.

If we had been there that day we likely would have missed it too, but for those of us who have the benefit of knowing the rest of the story, it's pretty clear what Jesus is saying here. Look closely at the twenty verses between 6:27 and 6:47 and see what word keeps popping up. The word is *believe.* How do we "work for the food that endures to eternal life" as Jesus instructed? He answers it there: "*Believe* in me!" Check out verse 35: "Whoever comes to me shall not hunger and whoever *believes* in me shall never thirst." Then hear it again in verse 40: "Everyone who *believes* in the Son shall have eternal life." And finally for emphasis in verse 47 he says, "Truly, truly, I say unto you, whoever believes in me shall have eternal life." I had an old Bible professor in college who used to say, "Whenever you see a 'truly, truly' from Jesus, it's basic gospel for dummies. It means, this is really, really true!"

For Jesus, eating is believing and drinking is believing. And he promises eternal life to those of us who believe this: that his death and sacrifice and spilling of his blood are God's exchange for our unrighteousness. In order for us to remember this new, true food, he tied it to the old food we know so well and hunger for on a daily basis. That's why the Lord's Supper is a big deal and always will be. He did not want us ever to forget the very core of what we are to believe.

Chapter Twenty-Five

THE LAST SUPPER

"Eating with the fullest pleasure is perhaps the profoundest enactment of our connection with the world."

—Wendell Berry

If there is a reason I wrote this book, it is this chapter. It is ironic, then, that it is likely here where I have the least to say. Far too many experts and scholars have plumbed theological depths around the Eucharist for a layman of my scant expertise to shed any new light on the subject. I will, however, stick to what I can do and offer a few stories and observations from my less-than-normal life that may (or may not) be of interest.

I was born into a Christian denomination that makes a big deal of the Lord's Supper. We took it every week without fail. It was, without a doubt, a sacrament for us, though we would never have used the word *sacrament* to refer to it or to any other religious activity.

We also believed strongly in the "priesthood of all believers," so it did not require a clergyman or priest to administer the holy Supper. At an appointed time in every Sunday morning service a few men would stand up around a table at the front of our worship area and one would say a prayer. Then they would pass the elements around. ("Elements." That's what we called them.) I heard Tony Campolo make a quip once that perfectly described our theological view of the Lord's Supper. Campolo said that in the centuries-old, deeply divided debate about transubstantiation and consubstantiation, his church (Baptists) sided with neither. They thought the bread remained bread and the wine, once consumed, made a trip past the lips and tongue and somewhere along the way was magically transformed into grape juice. Ha. That was us too—though, to be safe, we just started with Welch's Grape Juice from the beginning and decided that was close enough to whatever Jesus used.

Anyway, within our denomination we had suffered many divisions over many issues, including one splinter group called "one-cuppers." I came from a group that dispensed the grape juice in little individual cups, so we sort of felt sorry for these backwards, unenlightened one-cuppers. They argued that Jesus and his disciples obviously had just one cup at the original Last Supper, and who were we to randomly change this for our own convenience? Looking back, I now realize they had an excellent point. Not one worth fighting about quite as much as they did, but I suspect it was a better point to choose to be sticklers about than many of the other issues my group got up in arms about.

I gained quite a bit of sympathy for the one-cupper perspective when my wife and I joined a mission team and moved to Uganda, East Africa. Churches there did not have access to those nifty little plastic, individualized cups I had grown accustomed to in my youth, so they were quite happily "one-cupping" the Lord's Supper. It took some getting used to, to sit in a crowd of fifty to a hundred people and commune from one cheap plastic cup bought in the local market as the worshipers passed it from person to person. It went against everything I ever learned about germs. It accorded perfectly, however, with everything I ever learned about community in the church. Here is what I mean: it's easier (for me, anyway) to believe we are in this together, this adventure we call life, if we act like it. If, during a time-out of a heated ball game, my teammate next to me hands me the Gatorade bottle and I drink from it, that strikes me as fairly normal. If that same teammate, dirty, sweating, aching from the contest at hand, ceases to listen to the coach's instructions, admonishments, and encouragements, and instead turns his focus to carefully pouring my little sip of water into a tiny individualized cup, I think I might get the impression he was not that serious about either winning or being my teammate. Maybe that's uncharitable, and American males do tend to be too into sports analogies for their own good, but I can't shake the feeling that our institutionalized versions of the Lord's Supper are just efficient enough to facilitate a reoccurrence of missing the point.

Today I often sit in my church in North Carolina and long to take the Lord's Supper with my brothers and sisters in Uganda. It just strikes me as much more real and communal to have your brother or sister hand you a cup he has just drunk from and hear the words of Christ, "This is my blood, shed for you."

For those of you less familiar with the Christian tradition of the Lord's Supper, perhaps I should back up and explain how it came about. Like so many things about our faith, we stole it. Okay, we borrowed it, from the Jews who had been doing a similar meal for centuries. Jesus and his disciples were in Jerusalem for Passover and, as was the tradition, they gathered to eat the sacred Passover meal together. That meal celebrated how God had rescued his people from slavery in Egypt. This was the meaning of this ritual meal back then, and it still is the message of the meal when Jews eat it today. (If you have not been to a Passover meal, find a Jewish friend and wangle an invitation. It's awesome!)

As they entered Jerusalem for this particular Passover, Jesus had some inside knowledge that his friends did not. He knew this would be their last Passover together and that in the days just ahead their world would unravel when he was arrested, tried, and executed. He sent a couple of his men ahead to prepare a place for the holy meal, and they secured an upper room in town. Luke's Gospel reminds us that the Passover meal launched the celebration of both the Passover and the Feast of Unleavened Bread, which ran the week following Passover. "Prepare" here meant several things: finding a place that was in Jerusalem proper (as per 2 Chronicles 35:18), organizing the sacrifice of the lambs in the temple, cooking them, preparing the place, assembling side dishes and utensils, and procuring the wine. When evening came, Jesus and his twelve apostles gathered and reclined around a table to share the special holiday meal together (Luke 22:7–38).

As I have mentioned in previous chapters, Luke loved meals. This is his seventh meal scene in his Gospel and one of the most dramatic. Even though we call this the "Last Supper," surprisingly, two more meals are still to come in Luke's final chapter.

Sitting around a dinner table is a great place for friends to enjoy fellowship and reflect on life. As such, the setting of the Last Supper is an ideal setting for Jesus' final words to his disciples. Jesus makes it a meal to remember by choosing this time when the Jews paused to remember God's saving of Israel to discuss his sacrifice on behalf of his followers. Not only does this historical event form the basis of the future Lord's Supper, but he also predicts a betrayal, defines true leadership, promises authority to his disciples, and predicts Peter's failure—all while serving them bread and wine in the process.

While the events of what we now call the passion seem to unfold rapidly and spiral out of control for the disciples, they do not catch Jesus by surprise at all. This Passover meal is no exception. Even though the evening will prove to be fraught with emotion, he starts calmly by saying, "I have eagerly desired to eat this meal with you." I am told by my friends who are experts in biblical languages that he uses a Hebrew idiom here that literally says, "I have desired with desire." In modern English he may be saying something like, "I have been thinking about this meal for quite a while now. I have been longing for it. Planning for it. It's the last time I will ever eat a Passover with you."

If you grew up in church like I did, you might be tempted to super-spiritualize this moment. But imagine if you had a chance to gather your closest friends and let them know you will be gone in the coming days. Imagine sitting with friends with whom you have eaten hundreds and even thousands of meals and realizing that this is the last one. These days in church we'd have the ministry staff edit a tear-jerker video complete with highlights of our "mission trip," complete with shots of the feeding of the five thousand, the meal at Mary's and Martha's, and shots of Zacchaeus in the tree, all of them snapped by the disciples on their iPhones. Surely all of these scenes and many more are flashing through Jesus' mind as they eat that final Passover.

While I like to imagine the sappy scene above with Jesus' disciples totally in tune to the gravity of the moment, it appears they stayed in character to their normal selves and remained largely clueless. In his dinner speech, Jesus lets them know that one of them will betray him. This understandably sets off a series of one after another asking him, "Surely you don't mean me?"

On the way to the upper room that evening, the Twelve had been fussing about which of them was the greatest. In response to this petty argument, Jesus seizes the opportunity to contrast leadership in the world with the leadership he expects of them. In the world, he tells them, leadership involves people in charge exercising their power over others. Greatness, says Jesus here, is not to be defined by one's position or résumé, but by one's attitude and willingness to serve. "You are the ones who stood by me in my trials," he says, words that must have burned their collective consciences later when they realized how quickly they all deserted him.

The speech he gives them becomes increasingly intense and even sad. One of his culminating statements is, "I confer on you a kingdom so that you may sit and eat and drink with me at my table." I must have read this section of Scripture a hundred times before I ever saw this. Up to the very end, even in his final parting words, where economy and clarity are vitally important, food and drink language is on Jesus' lips. "When I sent you out with just a bag and some sandals, did you lack anything?" he asks them. "Nothing," they reply. He's referring to Luke 10, when he sent out the disciples, using harvest language. His instruction then was to "eat what is offered you" and to "stay there eating and drinking" in the homes of those whom they found "promoting peace." Now at the close of his time with them, Jesus promises them that if they lacked nothing then, they will not lack in the future either.

As he closes, they are strangely silent, except for Peter who, to his credit, boldly says, "I will go with you to prison and even death." A statement that proves false in the short run but prophetically true in the long run if church tradition about his death is accurate. Then it all ends. Their last supper is over. No sappy emotional slide show. It doesn't end like the disciples planned it or expected. But it does end exactly as Jesus knew it would all go down.

Now every week in my church we take the Lord's Supper, and even though I mentioned earlier how rote it becomes sometimes, I am intensely proud to be part of a crowd who takes this risk and eats it "as often as we come together." Perhaps we'd be more biblical if we used just one cup, but I much prefer the weekly observance to taking it every once in a while or whenever we get around to it.

When we gather around the Lord's Table each week, however, we would do well to remember that the Eucharist is not simply a one-dimensional production of the Body and Blood of Christ. It is a command to leave the church service to supply food for our brothers and sisters who are hungry. Monika Hellwig in her book, *The Eucharist and the Hunger of the World*, says it well:

> Basic hunger quickly broadens into the need for physical sustenance more generally—the need for warmth, cover, rest, clean air, and so on. But equally pervasive, equally important and far more subtle is the need to be loved into being and the hunger in which that need manifests itself.[1]

When we take the Lord's Supper, we should be careful that we don't approach it in search of meaning that can make it relevant for our modern times. Our strategy should be just the opposite, in fact. We should let it take us back to the ancient—to the most simple and elemental parts of our faith: hunger for God, longing to be filled, the need (not the obligation) to do his will. The sacrifice and mystery wrapped up in the Eucharist call us to a transformation from sin and selfishness and to life in Christ. This personal transformation is what the sacrifice is all about. The fact that God allows us this high church moment in the form of a simple meal with friends is so gracious of him. Just what we might expect from a God who loves to feed us.

Note

[1]Monica Hellwig, *The Eucharist and the Hunger of the World* (Landham, MD: Sheed & Ward, 1992), 8.

Chapter Twenty-Six

FEED MY SHEEP

"A mouthful of camel's milk keeps you going for half a day."

—Somali proverb

I am a child of the '80s. I graduated from high school in 1985. Unlike the styles of the '50s, '60s, and '70s that have all cycled back in and become cool with future generations of youth, I don't think the styles and trends of my high school years will ever pull that off. The mullet hair style for men was in. Boy George and Culture Club were chart toppers. Believe me, I have the pictures to prove it was forgettable stuff.

While the styles and much of the music of the '80s proved forgettable, one thing that happened in the fall of '84, my senior year, shaped us and has deeply impacted both us and generations to come. That event was the Ethiopian famine of 1984–85. The famine led to four hundred thousand deaths through a perfect storm of bad luck, bad weather, poor governance, and insurgency.

Our high schoolers were no more globally aware than any before us or since. In fact, in the case of my school, Kearsley High School in the blue-collar town of Flint, Michigan, we were almost certainly less globally aware than most. We went on about our lives, blissfully unaware of the suffering and the death sweeping through Ethiopia. Few if any of us could find Ethiopia on the map, and few if any of us cared what happened there, no matter how bad or unfair it may have been.

But during Christmastime of 1984 an obscure British musician named Bob Geldof saw the news reports coming out of Ethiopia and wrote a song called "Do They Know It's Christmas?" They recorded it and released it in an amazing four-day period in late November, going public with it under the name Band Aid. By Christmas that recording was topping charts in the United Kingdom and in the United States. The teenagers could not help themselves; the most popular song in the land was about the Ethiopia famine. When all was said and done, it raised eight million dollars. Nothing like this had ever been imagined or attempted before.

But it was just the beginning. Inspired by Geldof and his success, American rock stars led by musician and activist Harry Belafonte took note and formed their own group called

USA for Africa. Their song "We Are the World" was sung by a Who's Who of music stars in our country, and it smashed records in the spring of 1985. By the time I graduated in June, that recording had become the first single ever to go quadruple platinum and was the fastest-selling pop single in U.S. history. In all, it raised more than sixty-three million dollars for starving people in Ethiopia. Everyone knew "We Are the World." Everyone had a copy. Everyone could lip sync to the words. Suddenly it was hip for the youth of America to care about Africa. Our coolest rock stars had taken notice, so we did too.

But it wasn't over yet. A few months later, in July 1985, a huge concert was organized by Geldof that was to be for my generation what Woodstock had been nearly twenty years before. (I spoke negatively earlier about how forgettable Boy George was, but he apparently came up with the original idea for Live Aid.) My fellow teenagers and I would have been content if the concert held at London's Wembley Stadium and simulcast at JFK Stadium in Philadelphia had been about sex, drugs, and rock and roll, but it wasn't. It was about Ethiopia. It was about stopping the needless death due to famine and hunger. The concert was to be called "Live Aid."

Live Aid drew seventy thousand fans to Wembley and one hundred thousand more to JFK in Philadelphia. An estimated audience of 1.9 billion people across one hundred fifty nations watched it on satellite link-ups and television. The musicians who appeared rivaled those at Woodstock. The United States show featured Mick Jagger, Tom Petty, Madonna, and Bob Dylan, to name a few, while David Bowie, Freddie Mercury from Queen, Paul McCartney, and an emerging new band called U2 performed in London. The goal was to raise about two million dollars with the one-day event. Instead, it raised almost two hundred eighty-four million dollars when all was said and done. For his effort, Gelfdof was knighted by Queen Elizabeth. While his band, the Boomtown Rats, faded in obscurity, Geldof did not.

A young musician and lead singer from U2 named Bono was particularly impacted by his Live Aid experience and his relationship with the elder Geldof. Unable to shake it, he and his wife Ali took a month off in September of 1985 and volunteered with World Vision at Ajibar Camp in Ethiopia. He was forever changed by those thirty days. By 1987, U2 had become the voice of our generation and their *Joshua Tree* album the sound track of my college years. Since that time Bono, an avowed follower of Jesus, has redefined the term "rock star." Through his organization One Campaign, he has raised hundreds of millions of dollars to combat AIDS, hunger, and other issues. Most impressively, he has helped secure ninety-five billion dollars in debt relief for poor nations. Today, fifty million additional children are in school thanks to his work, and for the first time in a century, there is actually good news for many of the poor in our world.

So why all this time spent talking about rock stars and rock bands in the closing chapter of a book about Jesus? Let me cite a couple of reasons. First off, just as Bono wears those weird blue glasses, my worldview—my cultural glasses that I wear—were colored by the events above. I really have no choice but to tell it this way. It is, as the saying goes, "the way

I see it." Accordingly, I believe that since the church of the '80s and '90s was really not all that interested in feeding the hungry, God reached down and used that most self-centered, self-aggrandizing, drug-addicted, self-serving group of narcissists to do it. I mean, really . . . rock stars? Are these the geniuses or the moral leaders of our day? Yet it started with them. I believe God spoke to the youth of my generation because the youth were listening to those stars, and the church was doing such a lousy job that God could never get anyone's attention there. As Bono said in a now famous interview with Michka Assayas, "Religion can be the enemy of God. It's often what happens when God, like Elvis, has left the building."

The second and main reason I tell it this way is because it fits so well with Jesus' last words with his disciples, "Feed my sheep."

In the closing chapters of the Gospel of John, Jesus dies and his disciples all go fishing. They need some food, and this is how they know to get it, so returning to fishing makes sense. In chapter 21, Jesus walks up on the seashore and calls out to them in the boat. "Catching anything?" he asks. That's the obligatory question everyone asks a fisherman as they approach him, isn't it? "Nothing," they reply, offering the obligatory response every honest fisherman I have ever been with gives to that question.

"Try over there and you'll find some," he says. They do it, and their net is immediately so full that they can't drag it in. Peter famously jumps in and swims to shore while his buddies row the heavy boat about a hundred yards in to meet them.

By the time they arrive, a fire is going, and Jesus is cooking up some fish and bread.

Wouldn't you know that the God who loves to feed them wouldn't have it any other way? He does not sit them down in nice rows and preach to them. He does not give them printed manuscripts of every word he ever said so that future generations could get it all right. He just makes a fire and they eat breakfast together. They are hungry. They have been fishing all night. So he feeds them.

Then he does what he does best; he refuses to stop with just breakfast. He refuses to let them focus only on the whopping 153 fish they just caught. (Quite a financial windfall, though it was, for them.) Verse 15 says it clearly: ". . . when they had finished eating." He does not start until they have been fed. Then he hits Peter with a heavy charge.

"Simon, son of John, do you love me?" Dispensing with the nickname "Rock" that Jesus had given Peter, now he uses the fisherman's old name—his real name. Simon needs to see if he still wants and deserves that other name after his rather poor performance a few days before in the high priest's garden when he was afraid to admit to a maiden that he even knew Jesus.

"Yes," Peter assures him immediately. "I love you."

"Then feed my sheep," Jesus replies.

Again Jesus asks Peter the same question, "Simon, son of John, do you love me?"

Again Peter replies, "Lord, you know I love you."

Jesus repeats the charge, "Take care of my sheep."

Finally, a third time Jesus asks him, “Simon, son of John, do you love me?”

This time the Gospel says Peter is hurt by the question. Maybe it hurts him because he is thinking of his three denials that Jesus had predicted at the Last Supper. Peter now emphasizes his earlier reply, “Lord, you know all things. You know I love you.”

And, one more time, Jesus says simply, “Feed my sheep.”

While there is no doubt that Jesus’ call for Peter to be “pastoral” in caring for people would encompass more than just feeding literal food to everyone in Jesus’ name, there is also little doubt that part of the duties and expectation of a true servant of Jesus should include a passion for feeding hungry people. He did not say, “Teach them, Peter.” He did not say, “Inspire them to leadership, Peter.” He did not say, “Build huge fancy buildings, Peter.” Jesus simply said, “Feed my sheep.”

The cool thing about it is that Peter got the message. Wavering Peter became a rock! In fact, Peter became a rock star before any rock stars existed. And, like the Band Aid people of the ’80s, Peter was interested in debt relief and serving the poor and harnessing talent to make the world better. Christ’s church, built in those early years by Peter, has had its miscues through the centuries, but it has done more to help the poor and feed the hungry than any other institution in the history of the world. It’s a shame that in our lifetimes that same church watched while rock stars scurried to end a famine in Ethiopia and an AIDS crisis across the continent of Africa. I hope you share my hope that in the coming generations we will reclaim that turf and, instead of "Live Aid" being a rock concert in a few locations, it will be the living hands and feet of the resurrected Jesus empowering his church to carry out his final words to Peter: "Feed my sheep."

Chapter Twenty-Seven

WE HAD HOPED . . .

"Don't take another mouthful before you have swallowed what is in your mouth."

—African proverb

We know the end to the Emmaus story in the Bible. So it's difficult for us to enter into the disappointment and discouragement of the disciples as they walk that road and the resurrected Jesus meets them in disguise. "We had hoped," they say—some of the most powerful words in all of Scripture to me. They have just squandered three years of their lives. *They had hoped.* But now, three days after Calvary, hope had faded, and they were sadly sauntering down a road, lost in a fog of disbelief and disillusionment. At any moment Jesus could have pulled back the hood and said, "Surprise! Ha! It's me." He could have wowed them on the spot with a resurrection revelation, but he didn't. He gave them some space and some time to tell their story and to express their disappointment at being misled and abandoned by him. "What are you discussing together as you walk along?" he asked. It's almost funny, because when he asked another group of disciples a similar question in Mark 9, they were afraid to answer him, because they had been in a debate about which of them was the greatest. In that instance he had caught them jockeying for top spots, comparing who had the skills and talents and experience to serve in the higher offices of Jesus' coming kingdom. But with this pair on the road to Emmaus it was different. Positions of power, delusions of honor-to-come, dreams of popularity and wealth—all such discussions, hopes, and pretense—were long gone. Their king-to-be was dead.

Luke does a great job capturing the drama. "They stood still, their faces downcast." Jesus' question stopped them in their tracks. Just to think about it made them so sad. Then they asked, "Have you been hiding under a rock?" (Okay, that's my paraphrase of Scripture—but then again, he actually had been hiding under a rock of sorts for the last three days, hadn't he?) What they actually said was this: "Are you the only one in Jerusalem who has not heard about what happened to Jesus?"

No sooner was this question out of their mouths than the still-disguised Jesus set about explaining to them, "beginning with Moses and all the prophets, what was said in all the Scriptures concerning himself." As they approached the village where they were going, Jesus acted as if he had to go on down the road. But the disciples "urged him strongly" to stay with them. So he did. The Scripture says, "When he was at the table with them, he took the bread, gave thanks, broke it, and gave it to them." And then, at that moment, they realized who he was—the Bread of Life feeding them bread! As soon as they recognized him, he disappeared from their sight. "Were not our hearts burning within us while he talked with us on the road and opened up the Scriptures to us?" they said to each other.

The two men were so excited that they got up immediately and headed back to Jerusalem. There they found the eleven apostles assembled together and told them what had happened on the road. They emphasized how Jesus was recognizable to them only after he broke the bread. "While they were still talking about this, Jesus appeared and stood among them and said, 'Peace be with you.'" Scripture says they were freaked out by this (startled and troubled) and started thinking they were seeing a ghost. "Why are you troubled and why do doubts rise in your minds?" Jesus asked them. "Look at my hands and my feet. Does a ghost have flesh and bones?"

It was an incredible, surreal moment. I can only imagine that those who stood there in that room had that moment seared into their memories forever. Certainly it was one of the highlights of their incredible journey with Jesus. No writer could ask for a more climactic finish to a book or story, but Luke then penned about the most anticlimactic, out-of-place ending imaginable in the very next verse. At least, it seems that way to me. The next words of Jesus seem to me like something a Monty Python writer might write: The moment was so historic, yet his next words seem so mundane—"Do you have something to eat around here?" It makes me laugh out loud to read it. And the next line is just as funny because it's also so ordinary. "And they gave him some broiled fish. And he ate it."

That's it. That's basically the end of the story. There it ends. With a simple meal. With broiled fish. With a little bread. With a meal.

So there we have it. Maybe we, his modern disciples, should pick up there as well. With a little broiled fish or chicken. Maybe what we need most is not a program or a mission trip around the world. Maybe it's a meal. That's not enough for sure if it's where we stop. But it may well be the perfect place for us to start.